THE TEATIME
COOKBOOK

THE TEATIME
COOKBOOK

150 HOMEMADE CAKES, BAKES & PARTY TREATS

VALERIE FERGUSON

HERMES
HOUSE

This edition is published by Hermes House, an imprint of Anness Publishing Ltd, Hermes House, 88–89 Blackfriars Road, London SE1 8HA; tel. 020 7401 2077; fax 020 7633 9499

www.hermeshouse.com; www.annesspublishing.com

If you like the images in this book and would like to investigate using them for publishing, promotions or advertising, please visit our website www.practicalpictures.com for more information.

Publisher: Joanna Lorenz
Editorial Director: Judith Simons
Editor: Molly Perham
Series Designer: Bobbie Colgate Stone
Designers: Andrew Heath and Adelle Morris
Production Controller: Claire Rae

Recipes contributed by: Catherine Atkinson, Angela Boggiano, Janet Brinkworth, Kathy Brown, Carla Capalbo, Frances Cleary, Carole Clements, Trisha Davies, Roz Denny, Nicola Diggins, Joanna Farrow, Rafi Fernandez, Christine France, Sarah Gates, Shirley Gill, Rosamund Grant, Carole Handslip, Janine Hosegood, Sarah Lewis, Gilly Love, Lesley Mackley, Norma MacMillan, Maggie Mayhew, Norma Miller, Katherine Richmond, Anne Sheasby, Liz Trigg, Laura Washburn, Steven Wheeler, Elizabeth Wolf-Cohen, Jeni Wright.
Photography: Karl Adamson, Edward Allwright, Steve Baxter, Louise Dare, James Duncan, John Freeman, Ian Garlick, Michelle Garrett, Amanda Heywood, Janine Hosegood, David Jordan, Don Last, William Lingwood, Patrick McLeavey, Michael Michaels, Thomas Odulate, Polly Wreford.

ETHICAL TRADING POLICY

At Anness Publishing we believe that business should be conducted in an ethical and ecologically sustainable way, with respect for the environment and a proper regard to the replacement of the natural resources we employ. As a publisher, we use a lot of wood pulp to make high-quality paper for printing, and that wood commonly comes from spruce trees. We are therefore currently growing more than 750,000 trees in three Scottish forest plantations: Berrymoss (130 hectares/320 acres), West Touxhill (125 hectares/305 acres) and Deveron Forest (75 hectares/185 acres). The forests we manage contain more than 3.5 times the number of trees employed each year in making paper for the books we manufacture. Because of this ongoing ecological investment programme, you, as our customer, can have the pleasure and reassurance of knowing that a tree is being cultivated on your behalf to naturally replace the materials used to make the book you are holding. Our forestry programme is run in accordance with the UK Woodland Assurance Scheme (UKWAS) and will be certified by the internationally recognized Forest Stewardship Council (FSC). The FSC is a non-government organization dedicated to promoting responsible management of the world's forests. Certification ensures forests are managed in an environmentally sustainable and socially responsible way. For further information about this scheme, go to www.annesspublishing.com/trees

Previously published as *Afternoon Teas, Homemade Bakes & Party Cakes*

NOTES

Bracketed terms are intended for American readers.
For all recipes, quantities are given in both metric and imperial measures and, where appropriate, in standard cups and spoons. Follow one set of measures, but not a mixture, because they are not interchangeable.
Standard spoon and cup measures are level. 1 tsp = 5ml, 1 tbsp = 15ml, 1 cup = 250ml/8fl oz.
Australian standard tablespoons are 20ml. Australian readers should use 3 tsp in place of 1 tbsp for measuring small quantities.
American pints are 16fl oz/2 cups. American readers should use 20fl oz/2.5 cups in place of 1 pint when measuring liquids.
Electric oven temperatures in this book are for conventional ovens. When using a fan oven, the temperature will probably need to be reduced by about 10–20°C/20–40°F. Since ovens vary, you should check with your manufacturer's instruction book for guidance.
Medium (US large) eggs are used unless otherwise stated.
Main front cover image shows Red Grape & Cheese Tartlets – for recipe, see page 136

PUBLISHER'S NOTE

Although the advice and information in this book are believed to be accurate and true at the time of going to press, neither the authors nor the publisher can accept any legal responsibility or liability for any errors or omissions that may have been made nor for any inaccuracies nor for any loss, harm or injury that comes about from following instructions or advice in this book.

Contents

Introduction

Afternoon tea is a meal we don't often
have time for these days, which makes
it even more special when we do. In
these pages both beginners and more
experienced home bakers will find
inspirational ideas for every teatime
occasion. The book is divided into
three sections. The Basic Recipes and
Techniques section gives recipes for

the cake bases that are used later in the book – quick-mix sponge cake, Madeira cake, and rich fruit cake – as well as the different types of icing, marzipan, apricot glaze and sugar flowers. The helpful techniques pages provide step-by-step instructions for such things as preparing cake tins, making pastry and bottling preserves.

The second section of the book offers a superb collection of teatime recipes: cakes and gâteaux; cookies; pies and tarts; muffins, scones and breads; and jams, jellies and preserves. The third section is devoted to party cakes. Whether you are celebrating a birthday, a christening or Hallowe'en, you will be sure to find the ideal cake.

BASIC RECIPES AND TECHNIQUES

EQUIPMENT

To obtain the best results when making cakes, it is necessary to have a selection of good equipment.

A selection of useful items for cake making and decorating.

• Accurate weighing scales, measuring spoons and cups are available in both metric and imperial measurements. Always measure level when using spoons unless otherwise stated in the recipe.
• A set of mixing bowls in various sizes and a selection of wooden spoons are essential items. However, an electric hand-held beater will save time and make cake-making easier.
• Cake tins (pans); the most useful are round or square in sizes 15 cm/6 in, 20 cm/8 in and 25 cm/10 in.
• Cooling racks; at least two racks are useful for cake making and decorating.
• A serrated knife for cutting the cooled cake without it crumbling.

• Pastry brush for brushing cakes with apricot glaze.
• A heavy rolling pin for rolling out marzipan and sugarpaste icing.
• Pastry and small cookie cutters in various shapes and sizes for cutting sugarpaste icing shapes.
• A palette knife for spreading
• Piping bags and a variety of nozzles of different sizes and shapes (or you can use baking parchment cones with the nozzles).
• A turntable is not essential but makes icing much easier.
• Sable paintbrushes for painting fine details on to cakes.
• Silver cake boards for presenting decorated cakes.

SUCCESSFUL CAKE-MAKING

There are a few simple guidelines which must be followed to achieve the best results when making any cake.

• Always use the correct shape and size of tin (pan) for the recipe you have chosen and make sure it is properly prepared and lined.
• Check that you have all the necessary ingredients measured correctly and that they are at the right temperature before you start mixing.
• Ensure soft margarine is kept chilled in the refrigerator to maintain the right consistency. Leave butter out to reach room temperature.
• Sift all dry ingredients to help aerate the mixture and to disperse lumps.
• Use the correct sugar. Caster (superfine) sugar creams more easily with fats than granulated sugar, and is used where a fine and soft texture is required. Soft brown sugar is used when making heavier cakes.
• Use good quality fruit and peel for fruit cakes. Sometimes sultanas (golden raisins) can become hard if they stored for too long.
• When making cakes by hand, beat well with a wooden spoon until the mixture is light and glossy; scrape down the mixture from the sides of the bowl during beating with a plastic mixing spatula to ensure even mixing.
• If a cake is being made in a food processor or an electric mixer, be very careful not to overprocess or overbeat. Scrape down the batter with a plastic spatula during mixing.

• If ingredients have to be folded into a mixture, use a plastic spatula with a flexible blade.
• Level cake mixtures with a palette knife before baking.
• Check that your oven is preheated to the temperature that is stated in the recipe. Failure to do this will affect the rising of the cake and the cooking time.
• If the cake appears to be cooked before the given time, it may indicate that the oven is too hot; conversely, if it takes longer to cook, it means the oven is too cool.
• The temperature of the cake mixture can cause the cooking time to vary. If conditions are cold, the mixture will be cold and take longer to cook and if it is warm the cooking time will be slightly quicker.
• The surface of the cake should be evenly browned and level; if the cake is overcooked or risen to one side, then the heat in the oven is uneven or the oven shelf is not level.

PREPARING CAKE TINS

Lining a Shallow Cake Tin

Lining tins (pans) is important so that the cake comes out of the tin without breaking or sticking to the base of the tin. This method is simple, but essential.

1 Place the tin on a piece of baking parchment, draw around the base with a pencil and cut out the paper inside this line to fit tightly.

2 Grease the base and sides of the tin with melted lard or soft margarine. Grease the paper and then place it neatly into the tin. It is now ready for filling with the cake mixture.

3 To line the sides of a tin: Cut a strip of paper long enough to wrap around the outside of the tin and overlap by 4 cm/1½ in. It should be wider than the depth of the tin by 2.5 cm/1 in.

4 Fold the strip lengthways at the 2.5 cm/1 in point and crease. Snip at regular intervals from the edge to the crease along the fold. Line the side of the tin, with the snipped part of the strip on and overlapping the base. Press the bottom lining in (Steps 1 and 2).

5 For square and rectangular cake tins, fold the paper and crease it with your fingernail to fit snugly into the corners of the tin. Then press the bottom paper lining into place.

Lining a Deep Cake Tin

1 Place the tin (pan) on a double thickness of greaseproof paper or baking parchment. Draw around the base with a pencil. Cut out the marked shape with a pair of scissors.

2 Cut a strip of double-thickness greaseproof paper or baking parchment long enough to wrap around the outside of the tin, leaving a small overlap. It should stand 2.5cm/1in above the top of the tin.

3 Brush the base and sides of the tin with melted vegetable fat or oil. Place the double strip of paper inside the tin, pressing well against the sides and making sharp creases if it must fit into corners. Place the cut-out shape in the base of the tin and press it flat.

4 Brush the base and side papers well with melted vegetable fat or oil. Place a strip of double-thickness brown paper around the outside of the tin and tie securely with a string.

Line a baking sheet with three or four layers of brown paper and stand the tin on top.

Greasing and Flouring

For some cake recipes, the tin (pan) does not need to be lined with paper, but just greased, or sometimes greased and floured.

1 To grease a tin: If using butter or margarine, hold a small piece in kitchen paper (or use your fingers), and rub it all over the base and side of the tin to make a thin, even coating. If using oil, brush a small amount on with a pastry brush.

2 To flour a tin: Put a small scoop of flour in the centre of the greased tin. Tip and rotate the tin to coat the base and side. Shake out excess flour, tapping to dislodge any pockets.

Quick-mix Sponge Cake

Choose chocolate, lemon or orange flavouring for this light and versatile sponge cake, or leave it plain.

Makes 1 x 20 cm/8 in round or 168cm/7in square cake

INGREDIENTS
115 g/4 oz/1 cup self-raising (self-rising) flour
5 ml/1 tsp baking powder
115 g/4 oz/½ cup soft margarine
115 g/4 oz/½ cup caster (superfine) sugar
2 eggs

FOR THE FLAVOURINGS
Chocolate: 15 ml/1 tbsp unsweetened
   cocoa powder blended with 15 ml/1 tbsp
   boiling water
Lemon: 10 ml/2 tsp grated lemon rind
Orange: 15 ml/1 tbsp grated orange rind

1 Grease and line a 20 cm/8 in round tin (pan) or 18cm/7in square tin.

2 Preheat the oven to 160°C/325°F/ Gas 3. Sift the flour and baking powder into a bowl. Add the margarine, sugar and eggs with the chosen flavourings, if using.

3 Beat with a wooden spoon for 2–3 minutes. The mixture should be pale in colour and slightly glossy.

4 Spoon the mixture into the cake tin and smooth the surface. Bake in the centre of the oven for 30–40 minutes, or until a skewer inserted into the centre comes out clean.

5 Turn out on to a wire rack, remove the lining paper and leave to cool completely.

Madeira Cake

This is a richer basic cake which is ideal for decorating.

Makes 1 x 20 cm /8 in round or 18 cm/7 in square cake

INGREDIENTS
225 g/8 oz/2 cups plain (all-purpose) flour
5 ml/1 tsp baking powder
225 g/8 oz/1 cup butter or margarine, at room temperature
225 g/8 oz/generous 1 cup caster (superfine) sugar
grated rind of 1 lemon
5 ml/1 tsp vanilla essence (extract)
4 eggs

1 Preheat the oven to 160°C/325°F/ Gas 3. Grease and line a cake tin (pan). Sift the flour and baking powder into a bowl. Set the mixture aside.

2 Cream the butter or margarine, adding the caster sugar about 30 ml/ 2 tbsp at a time, until light and fluffy. Stir in the lemon rind and vanilla essence. Add the eggs, one at a time, beating for 1 minute after each addition. Add the flour mixture and stir until just combined.

3 Pour the cake mixture into the prepared tin and tap lightly to level. Bake for about 1¼ hours, or until a metal skewer inserted in the centre comes out clean.

4 Cool in the tin on a wire rack for 10 minutes, then turn the cake out and leave to cool completely.

Rich Fruit Cake

Make this cake a few weeks before icing, wrap well and store in an airtight container to mature.

Makes 1 x 20 cm/8 in round or 18 cm/7 in square cake

INGREDIENTS

375 g/13 oz/1¾ cups currants
250 g/9 oz/1½ cups sultanas (golden raisins)
150 g/5 oz/1 cup raisins
90 g/3½ oz/scant ½ cup glacé (candied) cherries, halved
90 g/3½ oz/scant 1 cup almonds, chopped
65 g/2½ oz/scant ½ cup mixed (candied) peel
grated rind of 1 lemon
40 ml/2½ tbsp brandy
250 g/9 oz/2¼ cups plain (all-purpose) flour
6.5 ml/1¼ tsp mixed (apple pie) spice
2.5 ml/½ tsp freshly grated nutmeg
65 g/2½ oz/generous ½ cup ground almonds
200 g/7 oz/scant 1 cup soft margarine or butter
225 g/8 oz/1 cup soft brown sugar
15 ml/1 tbsp black treacle (molasses)
5 eggs, beaten

1 Preheat the oven to 140°C/275°F/ Gas 1. Grease and line the base and sides of a 20 cm/8 in round or 18 cm/ 7 in square cake tin (pan) with a double thickness of baking parchment.

2 Sift the flour and combine with the other ingredients in a mixing bowl. Beat with a wooden spoon for 5 minutes. Spoon into the prepared tin. Make a slight depression in the centre.

3 Bake in the centre of the oven for 3–3½ hours. Test the cake after 3 hours. If it is ready it will feel firm, and a skewer inserted in the centre will come out clean. Cover the top loosely with foil if it starts to brown too quickly.

4 Leave to cool completely in the tin, then turn out. The lining paper can be left on to keep the cake moist.

Butter Icing

The creamy rich flavour and silky smoothness of butter icing is popular with both children and adults.

Makes 350 g/12 oz/1½ cups

INGREDIENTS
225 g/8 oz/2 cups icing (confectioners')
    sugar, sifted
75 g/3 oz/6 tbsp soft margarine or
    butter, softened
5 ml/1 tsp vanilla essence (extract)
10–15 ml/2–3 tsp milk

FOR THE FLAVOURINGS
Chocolate: Blend 15 ml/1 tbsp unsweetened
    cocoa powder with 15 ml/1 tbsp hot water.
    Cool before beating into the icing.
Coffee: Blend 10 ml/2 tsp coffee powder
    with 15 ml/1 tbsp boiling water. Omit the
    milk. Cool before beating the mixture into
    the icing.
Lemon, orange or lime: Replace the vanilla
    essence and milk with lemon, orange or
    lime juice and 10 ml/2 tsp finely grated
    citrus rind. Omit the rind if using the icing
    for piping. Lightly tint the icing with food
    colouring, if wished.

COOK'S TIP: Use Butter Icing for
fillings, toppings and as a thin
coating over a cake before adding
Sugarpaste Icing.
    The icing will keep for up to
3 days in an airtight container stored
in the refrigerator.

1 Put the icing sugar, margarine or butter, vanilla essence and 5 ml/1 tsp of the milk into a bowl.

2 Beat with a wooden spoon or an electric mixer until creamy. Add sufficient extra milk, a little at a time until the icing has a light, smooth and fluffy consistency.

3 To make flavoured butter icing, follow the instructions for chocolate, coffee or citrus flavourings given above for the flavour of your choice.

Marzipan

This can be used on its own, under an icing or for modelling.

Makes 450 g/1 lb/3 cups

INGREDIENTS
225 g/8 oz/2 cups ground almonds
115 g/4 oz/½ cup caster (superfine) sugar
115 g/4 oz/1 cup icing (confectioners') sugar, sifted
5 ml/1 tsp lemon juice
a few drops of almond essence (extract)
1 small (US medium) egg, or 1 medium (US large) egg white

1 Stir the ground almonds and caster and icing sugars together in a bowl until evenly mixed. Make a well in the centre and add the lemon juice, almond essence and enough egg or egg white to mix to a soft, but firm dough, using a wooden spoon.

2 Form the marzipan into a ball. Lightly dust a surface with icing sugar and knead the marzipan until smooth. Wrap in clear film (plastic wrap) or store in a polythene bag until needed.

Sugarpaste Icing

Sugarpaste (fondant) icing is wonderfully pliable and can be coloured, moulded and shaped.

Makes 350 g/12 oz/2¼ cups

INGREDIENTS
1 egg white
15 ml/1 tbsp liquid glucose, warmed
350 g/12 oz/3 cups icing (confectioners') sugar, sifted

1 Put the egg white and glucose in a mixing bowl. Stir them together to break up the egg white. Add the icing sugar and mix together with a palette knife, using a chopping action, until well blended and the icing begins to bind together. Knead the mixture with your fingers until it forms a ball.

2 Knead the sugarpaste on a work surface lightly dusted with icing sugar for several minutes until smooth, soft and pliable. If the icing is too soft, knead in some more sifted sugar until it reaches the right consistency.

Royal Icing

Use for a truly professional finish. This recipe makes enough icing to cover the top and sides of an 18 cm/7 in round cake.

Makes 675 g/1½ lb/4½ cups

INGREDIENTS
3 egg whites
about 675 g/1½ lb/6 cups icing
   (confectioners') sugar, sifted
7.5 ml/½ tsp glycerine
a few drops of lemon juice

2 Gradually add the icing sugar, beating well with a wooden spoon after each addition. Add enough icing sugar to make a smooth, shiny icing that has the consistency of very stiff meringue. Do not use an electric mixer as this will make the icing too fluffy.

1 Put the egg whites in a bowl and stir lightly with a fork or a wooden spoon to break them up.

COOK'S TIP: This recipe is for an icing consistency suitable for flat icing a marzipanned rich fruit cake. When the spoon is lifted, the icing should form a sharp point, with a slight curve at the end, known as "soft peak".

For piping, the icing needs to be slightly stiffer. It should form a fine sharp peak when the spoon is lifted. Add more icing (confectioners') sugar to achieve this consistency.

3 Beat in the glycerine and lemon juice. Leave for 1 hour, or up to 24 hours before using, covered with damp clear film (plastic wrap), then stir to burst any air bubbles.

Fudge Frosting

This rich, darkly delicious frosting can transform a simple sponge into an excitingly decorated novelty cake.

Makes 350 g/12 oz/2¼ cups

INGREDIENTS
50 g/2 oz/2 squares plain (semisweet) chocolate, chopped into small pieces
225 g/8 oz/1½ cups icing (confectioners') sugar, sifted
50 g/2 oz/¼ cup butter or margarine
45 ml/3 tbsp milk or single (light) cream
5 ml/1 tsp vanilla essence (extract)

1 Put the chocolate, icing sugar, butter or margarine, milk or cream and vanilla essence in a heavy pan.

2 Stir over a very low heat until the chocolate and butter or margarine melt. Remove from the heat and stir until evenly blended.

3 Beat the icing frequently as it cools until it thickens sufficiently to use for spreading or piping.

4 Use immediately and work quickly once it has reached the right consistency, otherwise it will be difficult to spread.

Glacé Icing

This icing can be made in just a few minutes and can be varied by adding a little food colouring or a flavouring such as coffee.

Makes 225 g/8 oz/1 cup

INGREDIENTS
225 g/8 oz/2 cups icing (confectioners') sugar
30–45 ml/2–3 tbsp warm water or fruit juice
food colouring or flavouring (optional)

1 Sift the icing sugar into a bowl. Using a wooden spoon, gradually stir in enough liquid to make an icing that is the consistency of thick cream.

2 Beat well until the icing is completely smooth. It should be thick enough to coat the back of the spoon. If it is too runny, beat in a little more sifted icing sugar.

3 Beat in a few drops of food colouring or flavouring, if using.

4 Use the icing immediately for coating or piping.

Apricot Glaze

Use the glaze to brush cakes before applying marzipan, or use for glazing fruits on gâteaux and cakes.

Makes 450 g/1 lb/1½ cups

INGREDIENTS
450 g/1 lb/1½ cups apricot jam
45 ml/3 tbsp water

1 Place the jam and water in a pan. Heat gently, stirring occasionally until melted. Boil rapidly for 1 minute.

2 Remove from the heat and rub through a sieve (strainer), pressing the fruit against the sides of the sieve with the back of a wooden spoon. Discard the skins left in the sieve.

3 Use a pastry brush to cover the entire surface of the cake.

Sugar-frosted Flowers

These pretty edible flowers may be used when a dainty and elegant decoration is required for a cake.

To cover about 20 flowers.

INGREDIENTS
Edible flowers, such as pansies, primroses, violets, roses, freesias or nasturtiums
1 egg white
caster (superfine) sugar

1 Trim the stems from the flowers leaving approximately 2 cm/¾ in if possible. Wash the flowers and dry gently on kitchen paper. Lightly beat the egg white in a small bowl and sprinkle some caster sugar on to a plate. Line another plate with kitchen paper.

2 Using a paintbrush, evenly brush both sides of the petals with the egg white. Holding the flower by the stem over the paper-lined plate, sprinkle it evenly with the sugar and shake off any excess.

3 Place on a flat board or wire rack covered with kitchen paper and leave to dry in a warm place.

COOK'S TIP: The flower stems are kept long for frosting so that they are easy to hold. They can be trimmed afterwards, if preferred.

SUCCESSFUL COOKIE-MAKING

Many cookies can be made from store cupboard items, but some will require fresh ingredients.

Dairy Products and Substitutes

Butter

Butter makes the richest cookies with the lightest texture. Use unsalted or lightly salted butter for sweet cookies. Margarine is also good, but tends to make more brittle biscuits. Low-fat spreads are suitable for many recipes, but do lack richness. They are useful for healthy eating and for those on a low-fat diet. Milk, yogurt, sour cream, cream and crème fraîche can all be used to bind the dough, giving slightly different flavours and textures.

Milk

Some cookies are filled or sandwiched together with cream. In such cases, use whipping or double (heavy) cream. Soft cheeses can also be used for fillings. Grated cheese is a wonderful flavouring for savoury biscuits. For best results, use hard or semi-hard cheeses, such as Parmesan or Cheddar. Eggs are also commonly used for binding the dough and, for best results, use free-range, organic eggs.

Parmesan Cheese

Eggs

Flour

Plain (all-purpose) flour is the most commonly used. For best results, choose organic stone-ground flour. Wholemeal (whole-wheat) flour is well-suited to savoury biscuits, while soft or sponge flour may be used on its own or mixed with plain flour for sweet cookies.

Fruit

Dried fruit is featured in many recipes and includes sultanas (golden raisins), raisins and apricots. The natural sugars add sweetness and moistness. Glacé (candied) cherries and candied fruit and peel may be used for decoration and also form an integral part of some cookies, such as florentines.

Dried Apricots

Sultanas

Glacé Cherries

Apart from very firm berries, fresh fruit is rarely used other than for decoration, as it tends to make cookies soggy. Fruit juices, however, can supply the flavour and natural sweetness of fresh fruit, so they are useful for binding the dough and flavouring fillings. Pear and apple spread, a concentrated fruit juice, is also excellent for binding and providing sweetness and flavour.

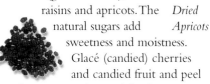

Flavourings

Unsweetened cocoa powder, plain (semisweet), milk or white chocolate and chocolate chips are widely used, both for flavouring and decoration. Grated citrus rind and vanilla and almond essences (extracts) feature in many recipes. Coffee, often as instant powder, is a popular flavouring. Brandy, whisky and liqueurs add sophisticated flavours to cookies.

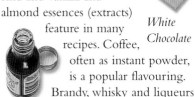

Plain Chocolate

White Chocolate

Vanilla Essence

Grains

Rolled oats and oatmeal feature in many traditional recipes. Corn meal makes lovely golden cookies. Muesli and breakfast cereals are also useful.

Oats

Herbs and Spices

Chopped fresh herbs may be used to add interest, particularly to savoury cookies. Common spices for sweet cookies are ground cinnamon, nutmeg and ginger. Savoury biscuits may also include spices or curry powder.

Ground Cinnamon

Nuts and Seeds

Traditional favourites are coconut, usually desiccated (shredded), walnuts, hazelnuts, pecan nuts, almonds and pine nuts. Seeds, such as sesame, sunflower and poppy, may be added to sweet cookies or savoury biscuits. They give additional texture, flavour and nutrients.

Hazelnuts

Sweeteners

Caster (superfine) sugar is easily incorporated into dough, although granulated is sometimes suggested. Unrefined sugars, such as soft dark brown sugar, have more flavour, add colour and contain some minerals. Honey has a strong flavour and is sweeter than sugar, so you can use less of it than the equivalent of sugar. Black treacle (molasses) has a smoky flavour and slightly bitter taste. It goes well with other strong flavours, such as ginger. Malt extract is also distinctive and is a good choice for softer bakes, as it adds moistness. Golden, corn and maple syrup are very sweet with a more subtle flavour. Always use pure maple syrup for the best flavour. Syrup is essential for some very light cookies, such as crisp brandy snaps.

Muscovado Sugar

Honey

COOKIE-MAKING TECHNIQUES

Stencilling

Use stencils to liven up cookies in a simple and fun way.

Cut a small design or initial out of card and place it over a cookie. Dust with icing (confectioners') sugar or cocoa before removing the card.

Grinding Nuts

Using a nut mill or a clean coffee grinder, grind a small batch of nuts at a time to ensure an even texture. As soon as the nuts have a fine texture, stop grinding; if overworked, they will turn to paste. Alternatively, use a food processor. To avoid overworking the nuts add some of the sugar or flour needed in the recipe.

Roasting Nuts

Roasting nuts brings out their flavour and makes them crunchier.

1 To oven-roast or grill (broil) nuts: spread the nuts on a baking sheet. Roast in a 180°C/350°F/Gas 4 oven or under a medium grill (broiler), until golden brown and smelling nutty. Stir the nuts to brown evenly.

2 To dry-roast nuts: put the nuts in a frying pan, with no fat. Roast over moderate heat until golden brown. Stir constantly and watch carefully: nuts can scorch easily.

COOK'S TIP: Set the timer for 3-4 minutes when oven-roasting nuts.

Melting Chocolate

There are basically three simple ways to melt chocolate:

Melting Over Hot Water

1 Fill a pan about a quarter full with water. Place a heatproof bowl on top. The water should not touch the bowl. Bring the water to simmering point, then lower the heat.

2 Break the chocolate into squares and place in the bowl. Leave to melt completely, without stirring. Keep the water at a very low simmer.

COOK'S TIP: The melted chocolate should be only just warm and never allowed to boil. Also, ensure that no water gets into the bowl.

Melting in the Microwave

Break the chocolate into squares and place it in a microwave-safe bowl. Heat in the microwave until just softened, checking frequently.

Approximate times for melting in a 650–700 watt microwave oven:
115 g/4 oz plain (semisweet) or milk
  2 minutes on High (100% power)
115 g/4 oz white chocolate
  2 minutes on Medium (50% power)

Direct Heat Method

This is only suitable where the chocolate is melted in plenty of liquid. Add the broken chocolate to the liquid in the pan, then heat gently, stirring occasionally, until the chocolate has melted and the mixture is smooth.

TYPES OF PASTRY

Shortcrust Pastry

One of the easiest and most versatile of pastries, shortcrust consists of flour and fat, with just enough liquid to bind the ingredients together. Always use iced water and, if time permits, wrap the pastry in clear film (plastic wrap) and chill it in the refrigerator for 30 minutes before rolling it out.

Rich or Sweet Shortcrust Pastry

Rich or sweet shortcrust pastry sets to a crisper crust than plain shortcrust. It is often used for fruit pies. Use the shortcrust recipe but use butter and substitute an egg yolk for part of the liquid. For sweet pastry, add 30–45 ml/2–3 tbsp caster (superfine) sugar after rubbing in the fat.

Below: Pear Tarte Tatin with Cardamom

Puff Pastry

This is made in such a way that it separates into crisp layers when cooked, thanks to the air trapped in it. A block of butter is wrapped in a basic dough, the pastry is then turned, rolled, folded and chilled several times. If using frozen puff pastry, thaw slowly.

Rough Puff Pastry

Diced fat is mixed with the flour but not rubbed in, so the fat can be seen in the dough. The pastry is rolled and folded several times before being rested and baked. The fat used should be very cold and it helps if the flour is chilled.

Choux Pastry

The butter is melted with water and then the flour added all at once and beaten in before the eggs. It is easy to make, but must be carefully measured.

PASTRY-MAKING TECHNIQUES

Rubbing In

Add the diced fat to the flour. Using the fingertips and thumbs, draw up a small amount of mixture and rub together to break it down into crumbs. Repeat the process lifting the mixture each time to incorporate air, until no large lumps of fat remain. Do not overwork the dough.

Using a Pastry Blender

A pastry blender is a gadget comprising between five and eight arched wires on a wooden handle. Some cooks prefer it for rubbing in as it stops warm hands softening the fat, but it can break down the fat almost too efficiently. Use the blender for half the fat, and add the rest in pea-size pieces.

Rolling Out

A smooth layer of pastry that will not distort or shrink in baking is the desired result. The key to successful rolling out is to handle the dough gently.

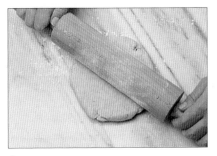

1 Using an even pressure, roll out the dough on a lightly floured surface. Start in the centre of the dough and roll out towards the edge.

2 Give the dough a quarter turn from time to time during the rolling, so that it rolls out evenly and does not stick to the surface. Continue the rolling out process until the dough circle is about 5 cm/2 in larger than the size of the tin. It should be about 3 mm/ ⅛ in thick.

Lining a Tin

Set the rolling pin on the dough, near one side. Fold the outside edge over the pin, then roll the pin to wrap the dough around it. Hold over the tin (pan) and unroll the dough into the tin. Lift and ease the dough into the tin, gently pressing the base and side. Turn excess dough over the rim and trim it with a knife or scissors.

Crimping a Pastry Shell

Make a "V" with the thumb and forefinger of one hand, pressing lightly on the pastry. Then use the index finger of your other hand to push between the "V" inwards. Or press the knuckle of one hand against the inner edge, using the other hand to pinch around your finger.

Glazing

For a rich, golden crust, brush the pastry with beaten egg, a mixture of beaten egg and water, or milk just before baking. For a sweet pie, you can add a light dusting of caster (superfine) sugar on top of the glaze.

Baking Blind

This refers to the method of partially or fully baking an unfilled pastry case. Line it with baking parchment and add an even layer of baking beans (use dried beans kept for the purpose or special china beans). Bake the case for 10 minutes, then remove the paper and baking beans and return the pastry case to the oven for 5 minutes more, or longer if it is not to be cooked again after filling.

Making Shortcrust Pastry

Use half butter or margarine and half
white vegetable fat, or all the same fat.

Lines a 23 cm/9 in pastry case

INGREDIENTS
225 g/8 oz/2 cups plain (all-purpose) flour
1.5 ml/¼ tsp salt
115 g/4 oz/½ cup fat, chilled and diced
45–60 ml/3–4 tbsp iced water

1 Sift the flour and salt into a bowl,
raising the sieve to incorporate as
much air as possible. Add the fat. Rub
into the flour until the mixture
resembles breadcrumbs.

2 Sprinkle 45 ml/3 tbsp water over.
Toss the mixture with your fingers to
combine and moisten.

3 Press the dough into a ball. If it is
too dry, add the remaining water.

4 Shape the dough into an oblong or
oval then wrap in clear film (plastic
wrap) and chill in the refrigerator for
30 minutes before using.

Making Puff Pastry

Puff pastry has a feather-light texture
because of its high butter content.

Makes 500 g/1¼ lb

INGREDIENTS
200 g/7 oz/⅞ cup unsalted (sweet) butter
200 g/7 oz/1½ cups fine plain
   (all-purpose) flour
1.5 m/l¼ tsp salt
125 ml/4 fl oz/½ cup cold water

1 Cut the butter into 14 pieces and
place in the freezer for 30 minutes.

2 Put the flour and salt in a food
processor and pulse to combine. Add
the butter and pulse three times; there
should still be large lumps of butter.
Run the machine for 5 seconds while
pouring the water through the feed
tube, then stop the machine. The
dough should look curdy.

3 Turn the mixture on to a lightly
floured, cool work surface and gather
into a flat ball. If the visible butter is
soft, chill the dough for 30 minutes.

4 Roll out the dough on a floured
surface to a 40 x 25 cm/16 x 6 in
rectangle. Fold in thirds, bringing one
end down to cover the middle, then
fold the other end over it. Roll out
again to a rectangle and fold again.
Chill for 30 minutes. Roll and fold
twice more then chill for 30 minutes.

BREAD INGREDIENTS

Above: A range of flours used for bread.

Flour White flour has a high gluten content, absorbs water readily and produces an elastic dough when kneaded. Strong white flour, made from hard wheat with a high proportion of gluten, is specifically for bread making. Wholemeal (whole-wheat) flour, containing the complete wheat kernel, produces coarser-textured bread with a high fibre content and a stronger flavour. Rye flour is dark and quite dense. It is often mixed with strong wheat flour to give a lighter loaf. Granary flour is a proprietary name given to a mixture of brown and rye flour and malted wheat grain.

Leavening Agents These all work on similar principles. When activated, carbon dioxide is produced and this makes the dough expand, trapping air in tiny pockets throughout. When the bread is baked, the air is locked in, making it light in texture.

Yeast is the traditional leavening agent. Fresh yeast is said to produce the best flavour. It requires warmth to make it work, but over-heating will kill it. Store it in the refrigerator. Dried yeast requires a preliminary mixing with lukewarm liquid. Dough made with fresh or dried yeast requires two sessions of proving (setting aside to increase in bulk). Easy-blend (rapid-rise) dried yeast can be added directly to the dry ingredients for the dough, which requires only a single proving.

Baking powder is an effective raising agent when added to plain (all-purpose) flour. Bicarbonate of soda (baking soda) is activated by acid, such as buttermilk. They both start working immediately they are combined with liquid and the dough does not require proving.

Salt An essential ingredient in yeast breads, salt stops the yeast from working too quickly.

Sweeteners A little sugar is usually added to fresh yeast to give it a good start. It is not needed with easy-blend dried yeast. As sugar slows down the action of yeast, sweet dough may need extra yeast and longer proving.

Honey may also be used in sweet breads. Malt extract, a sugary by-product of barley, has a strong flavour and adds moistness. Molasses or black treacle, by-products of sugar refining, have a strong, smoky, slightly bitter taste.

Above: Granary (top), wholemeal and white breads make excellent toast.

Liquid Water is the liquid most often used in bread-making, but milk is also popular. It should be lukewarm for yeast dough. Quantities in recipes are for guidance, as flours vary in how much they will absorb.

Flavourings Sweet and savoury flavourings may be incorporated in the dough while kneading. These include sautéed onions, celery or courgettes (zucchini), sun-dried tomatoes, fresh or dried herbs, ground spices, cheese, dried fruit, glacé (candied) cherries, candied peel and chopped nuts. Be careful when adding ingredients with a high fat content, such as cheese, as too much will spoil the texture of the bread. Nuts, dried fruits, seeds, vegetables and grated cheese may also be used as toppings. Adding oil, butter or margarine to the dough improves

the softness of the crumb and delays staleness. Too much, however, impairs the action of the yeast.

Eggs Eggs add flavour and colour and have the benefit of improving the keeping quality of rich breads.

Above: A selection of white breads.

33

BREAD-MAKING TECHNIQUES

Using Fresh Yeast Crumble into a small bowl, add a pinch of sugar and cream the mixture with lukewarm water. Set aside in a warm place for 5–10 minutes, until frothy. Add to the dry ingredients.

Using Dried Yeast Sprinkle on to lukewarm liquid, preferably water, and add a pinch of sugar. Stir and set aside for 10–15 minutes, until frothy. Add to the dry ingredients.

Using Easy-blend Dried Yeast Add straight from the sachet to the dry ingredients. Mix the dough with lukewarm liquid.

Sponging Dissolve the yeast in more lukewarm water than usual, then mix with some of the flour to make a batter. Set aside for a minimum of 20 minutes, until bubbles appear. Mix with the remaining flour.

A Few Simple Rules
- Warm bowls and equipment.
- For lukewarm water (37–43°C/ 98–108°F), mix two parts cold with one part boiling water.
- Knead the dough for at least 10 minutes to stretch the gluten and produce a light-textured loaf.
- Do not leave the dough to prove in a draught.
- Cover the dough while proving to keep it moist.

Adding Fats Add diced butter or margarine to the dry ingredients and rub in with the fingertips until the mixture resembles breadcrumbs. Add oil with the liquid.

Kneading by Hand Turn the dough out on to a lightly floured surface. With floured hands, fold it towards you, pulling and stretching, then push it down firmly with the heel of your hand. Give it a quarter turn and repeat the action for about 10 minutes, until the dough is smooth, elastic and no longer sticky.

Kneading in a Food Processor Do not try to knead more dough than recommended by the manufacturer. If necessary, knead in batches. Fit the dough blade and blend together the dry ingredients. Add the yeast mixture, lukewarm liquid, oil or butter, if using, and process until the mixture comes together. Knead for 1 minute, or according to the manufacturer's instructions. Turn out and knead by hand for 1–2 minutes.

Kneading in a Mixer Mix the dry ingredients. Add the yeast mixture, liquid, oil or butter, if using, and mix slowly with the dough hook until the mixture comes together. Continue for 3–4 minutes, or according to the manufacturer's instructions.

Proving This is the process of setting the dough aside in a warm place to increase in bulk. Keep it moist by covering it with a damp dishtowel or lightly oiled clear film (plastic wrap). A loaf or rolls on a baking sheet can be slipped inside a plastic bag, ballooned to trap the air. Set aside in a warm place (24–27°C/75–80°F) for an hour or more, until doubled in bulk.

Shaping Rolls To make cottage rolls, shape two-thirds of the dough into rounds the size of golf balls and the remainder into smaller rounds. Make a dent in each large ball and press a small ball on top.

To make knots, roll each dough portion into a fairly thin sausage and knot it like string.

To make twists, twist two strands of dough, dampen the ends and seal.

To make clover-leaf rolls, divide each portion of dough into three equal pieces. Dampen lightly and fit in a bun tin, if liked, pressing lightly to hold.

To make braids, divide each portion of dough into three equal pieces and roll them into sausages. Dampen them at one end and press together. Braid loosely, dampen the other end and press together.

To make snipped-top rolls, roll each portion of dough into a smooth ball. Snip the top with kitchen scissors.

Glazing Glazing can give an attractive finish and introduces moisture during cooking. Bread may be glazed before, during or just after baking. Glazes include egg yolk, egg white, milk, butter, sugar or salt solutions and olive oil. Take care not to brush glazes up the sides of a tin (pan) or drip on a baking sheet, otherwise the bread will stick and crack.

Topping Roll dough in a topping before the second proving or glaze and sprinkle just before baking. Popular toppings include cheese, oats, cracked wheat, sea salt, sunflower, sesame, poppy or caraway seeds, herbs, corn meal and wheat flakes.

Testing Bread
1 At the end of the cooking time, loosen the edges of the loaf with a metal spatula and turn out.

2 Hold the loaf upside down and tap it gently on the base. If it sounds hollow, the bread is ready.

SUCCESSFUL JAM-MAKING

Choosing Containers

Glass jars and bottles are a popular
choice for all kinds of preserves
because they are durable, versatile and
decorative, enhancing the appearance
of their contents. Modern recycled
glass has many of the qualities of
antique glass, such as flaws and
colourings, and is inexpensive.

Earthenware jars and pots are also good
choices for chutneys and home-made
mustards. Specially made preserving jars
are best for bottled fruit and vegetables
and can be reused, although you should
always use fresh seals.

Sterilizing

To ensure that harmful bacteria are
eliminated, it is essential to sterilize
bottles and jars and their lids, if they
have them. This can be done in a
variety of ways.

To sterilize in the oven, stand the
containers on a baking sheet lined
with newspaper or on a wooden
board and rest their lids on them, but
do not seal. Make sure they are not
touching. Place them in a cold oven
and then turn it on to 110°C/225°F/
Gas ¼ and leave the containers for
30 minutes. This method has the
advantage of ensuring the containers
are warm when they are filled with
hot jam, syrup or chutney; otherwise
they would crack. If you are not going
to use them immediately, cover with a
clean cloth and make sure they are
warmed again before being filled.

An alternative method is to put
the containers and their lids in a
dishwasher and run it on its hottest
setting, including the drying cycle, but
without adding any detergent. This,
too, ensures the containers are warm
when they are filled.

It is also necessary to sterilize a jelly
bag before use. Set the bag over a large
bowl and pour boiling water through
it. Discard the water and replace the
bowl with a clean one.

Seals and Labels

The type and effectiveness of the seal required depend on the kind of preserve and the process used. Jams and jellies can be covered with a disc of baking parchment and the top of the jar covered with paper or cellophane held in place with an elastic band. Bottled fruit and vegetables must be sealed with new rubber seals and the lids clipped in place. Chutneys and pickles should be sealed with vinegar-proof lids that will not corrode.

Ideally, all preserves should be labelled with a description of the contents and the date they were made. Self-adhesive labels may be attached to the surface of the container or wooden or metal labels may be tied around the neck.

Setting Point

To test jams and jellies for the setting point, spoon a small quantity on to a chilled saucer. Chill for 3 minutes, then push the jam with your finger. If wrinkles form on the surface, the jam is ready. Alternatively, you could use a sugar thermometer clipped to the side of the pan, but not touching the base. When the temperature reaches 105°C/220°F, the jam is ready.

Most jams will benefit if left to stand for about 15 minutes before being ladled into jars. This ensures that the pieces of fruit are evenly distributed. A jam funnel is useful for preventing hot spillages; it can also be used when filling jars with chutney.

Teatime Treats and Fancy Bakes

Afternoon tea is one of the most delightful occasions – it provides an excellent opportunity to try out your home baking skills, and you can prepare the food in advance so that you are free to sit down and chat with your guests. A special cake may well be the centrepiece of your tea-table, and you will find several traditional recipes,

such as Victoria Sandwich and Dundee Cake, as well as more exotic and unusual gâteaux. The pies and tarts section offers tempting recipes made from shortcrust or puff pastry – either make your own or save time and buy the ready-made version. There is also a section on muffins, scones and interesting breads, and a selection of recipes for jams and jellies to spread on them. Cookies are quick and easy to make and keep well, so you can always have a good supply ready for when unexpected guests drop in. The following pages provide plenty of ideas to inspire your home baking and enable you to serve an afternoon tea that everyone will remember.

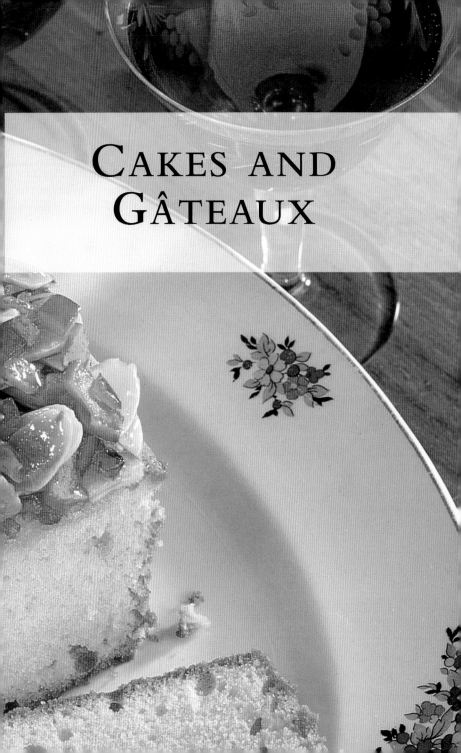

CAKES AND
GÂTEAUX

One-stage Victoria Sandwich

This melt-in-the-mouth sponge is easy and quick to make.

Serves 6–8

INGREDIENTS
175 g/6 oz/1½ cups self-raising
   (self-rising) flour
pinch of salt
175 g/6 oz/¾ cup butter, softened
175 g/6 oz/¾ cup caster (superfine) sugar
3 eggs

TO SERVE
60–90 ml/4–6 tbsp raspberry jam
icing (confectioners') sugar

1 Preheat the oven to 180°C/350°F/
Gas 4. Grease two deep 18 cm/7 in
cake tins (pans), line the bases with
baking parchment and lightly grease
the paper itself.

2 Place the ingredients in a mixing
bowl and whisk together using a
hand-held whisk. Divide the mixture
between the prepared tins and smooth
the surfaces.

3 Bake in the centre of the oven for
25–30 minutes, or until a skewer
inserted into the centre of the cakes
comes out clean. Turn out on to a
wire rack, peel off the lining paper and
leave to cool completely.

4 Place one of the cakes on a
serving plate and spread with the
raspberry jam. Place the other cake
on top, then dredge with icing
(confectioners') sugar, to serve. Use a
stencil to make a pattern, if liked.

Honey Spice Cake

Use a strongly flavoured honey, such as chestnut honey, for this cake.

Serves 8–10

INGREDIENTS

150 g/5 oz/⅔ cup butter
115 g/4 oz/½ cup soft light brown sugar
175 g/6 oz/¾ cup clear honey
15 ml/1 tbsp water
200 g/7 oz/1¾ cups self-raising (self-rising)
   flour, sifted
2.5 ml/½ tsp ground ginger
2.5 ml/½ tsp ground cinnamon
1.5 ml/¼ tsp caraway seeds
1.5 ml/¼ tsp ground cloves
2 eggs, beaten
350 g/12 oz/3 cups icing (confectioners')
   sugar, sifted
crushed sugar, to decorate

1 Preheat the oven to 180°C/350°F/
Gas 4. Grease a 900 ml/1½ pint/
3¾ cup fluted mould.

2 Melt the butter in a pan with the
sugar, honey and water. Cool.

3 Mix the flour, ginger, cinnamon,
caraway seeds and ground cloves in a
bowl. Pour in the honey mixture and
the eggs and beat well. Pour the batter
into the tin and bake for 45 minutes,
until a skewer inserted into the centre
comes out clean. Cool in the tin for 2
minutes, then remove to a wire rack.

4 Mix the icing sugar with warm
water to make the icing. Spoon over
the cake. Decorate with crushed sugar.

Crunchy-topped Madeira Cake

Traditionally served with a glass of Madeira wine in Victorian England, this light sponge also makes a perfect teatime treat.

Serves 8–10

INGREDIENTS
200 g/7 oz/scant 1 cup butter, softened
finely grated rind of 1 lemon
150 g/5 oz/⅔ cup caster (superfine) sugar
3 eggs
75 g/3 oz/⅔ cup plain (all-purpose) flour
150 g/5 oz/1¼ cups self-raising
    (self-rising) flour

FOR THE TOPPING
45 ml/3 tbsp clear honey
115 g/4 oz/¾ cup chopped mixed peel
50 g/2 oz/½ cup flaked (sliced) almonds

1 Preheat the oven to 180°C/350°F/ Gas 4. Grease and line a 450 g/1 lb loaf tin (pan) and grease the paper.

2 Beat the butter, lemon rind and sugar in a bowl until light and fluffy. Beat in the eggs, one at a time.

3 Sift together the flours, then stir into the egg mixture. Transfer the cake mixture to the prepared tin and smooth the surface.

4 Bake in the centre of the oven for 45–50 minutes, or until a skewer inserted into the centre of the cake comes out clean. Leave the cake in the tin for about 5 minutes. Turn out on to a wire rack, peel off the lining paper and leave to cool completely.

5 To make the topping, place the honey, mixed peel and almonds in a small pan and heat gently until the honey melts.

6 Remove from the heat and stir briefly to coat the peel and almonds, then spread over the cake. Allow to cool completely before serving.

Carrot Cake

This deliciously sweet and light-textured cake – which doesn't taste of carrots – is covered with an unusual frosting made with soft cheese.

Makes a 20 cm/8 in round cake

INGREDIENTS
250 ml/8 fl oz/1 cup corn oil
175 g/6 oz/scant 1 cup sugar
3 eggs
175 g/6 oz/1½ cups plain (all-purpose) flour
7.5 ml/1½ tsp baking powder
7.5 ml/1½ tsp bicarbonate of soda (baking soda)
3 ml/¾ tsp salt
7.5 ml/1½ tsp ground cinnamon
a pinch of freshly grated nutmeg
1.5 ml/¼ tsp ground ginger
115 g/4 oz/1 cup chopped walnuts
225 g/8 oz (2 large) carrots, finely grated
5 ml/1 tsp vanilla essence (extract)
30 ml/2 tbsp sour cream

FOR THE FROSTING
175 g/6 oz/¾ cup full-fat soft cheese
25 g/1 oz/2 tbsp butter, softened
225 g/8 oz/2 cups icing (confectioners') sugar, sifted
8 tiny carrots made from orange and green coloured marzipan, to decorate

1 Preheat the oven to 180°C/350°F/Gas 4. Grease two 20 cm/8 in loose-based round cake tins (pans) and line them with baking parchment.

2 Put the corn oil and sugar into a bowl and beat well. Add the eggs, one at a time, and beat them very thoroughly into the mixture.

3 Sift the flour, baking powder, bicarbonate of soda, salt, cinnamon, nutmeg and ginger into the bowl and beat well. Fold in the walnuts and carrots and stir in the vanilla essence and sour cream.

4 Divide the mixture between the prepared tins and bake in the centre of the oven for about 1 hour 5 minutes, or until a skewer inserted into the centre of the cake comes out clean.

5 Leave the cake in the tins for 5 minutes then turn out to cool on a wire rack. For the frosting mix the soft cheese, butter and icing sugar together in a bowl. Beat until smooth.

6 Sandwich the cooled cakes together with a little of the frosting. Spread the remaining frosting over the top of the cake and down the sides, making a swirling pattern with a round-bladed knife. Just before you are ready to serve the cake, decorate the top with the orange and green marzipan carrots, arranged in an attractive pattern.

47

Passion Cake

So called because this is a cake associated with Passion Sunday. The carrot and banana give the cake a rich, moist texture.

Serves 6–8

INGREDIENTS

200 g/7 oz/1¾ cups self-raising (self-rising) flour
10 ml/2 tsp baking powder
5 ml/1 tsp cinnamon
2.5 ml/½ tsp freshly grated nutmeg
150 g/5 oz/⅔ cup butter, softened, or sunflower margarine
150 g/5 oz/⅔ cup soft brown sugar
grated rind of 1 lemon
2 eggs, beaten
2 carrots, coarsely grated
1 ripe banana, mashed
115 g/4 oz/¾ cup raisins
50 g/2 oz/½ cup chopped walnuts or pecans
30 ml/2 tbsp milk
6–8 walnuts, halved, to decorate
coffee crystal sugar, to sprinkle

FOR THE FROSTING

200 g/7 oz/scant 1 cup cream cheese, softened
40 g/1½ oz/⅓ cup icing (confectioners') sugar
juice of 1 lemon
grated rind of 1 orange

1 Line and grease a deep 20 cm/8 in round cake tin (pan). Preheat the oven to 180°C/350°F/Gas 4. Sift the flour, baking powder, cinnamon and freshly grated nutmeg together into a large mixing bowl.

2 Using an electric mixer, cream the butter or margarine and sugar with the lemon rind until it is light and fluffy, then beat in the eggs. Fold in the flour mixture, then the carrots, banana, raisins, nuts and milk.

3 Spoon the mixture into the prepared tin, level the top and bake for about 1 hour, until it has risen and the top is springy to touch. Turn the tin upside down and allow the cake to cool in the tin for 30 minutes. Transfer the cake to a wire rack.

4 When cold, split the cake in half. Cream the cheese with the icing sugar, lemon juice and orange rind, then sandwich the two halves together with half the frosting.

5 Spread the rest of the frosting on top of the cake, swirling it attractively with a knife. Decorate the top with the walnut halves and sprinkle with coffee crystal sugar.

49

Dundee Cake

This traditional rich fruit cake is topped with a mixture of nuts and glacé cherries and tastes every bit as good as it looks.

Serves 8–10

INGREDIENTS
350 g/12 oz/3 cups plain wholemeal
    (whole-wheat) flour
5 ml/1 tsp mixed (apple pie) spice
175 g/6 oz/¾ cup unsalted (sweet) butter
175 g/6 oz/¾ cup dark
    muscovado sugar
175 g/6 oz/1 cup sultanas (golden raisins)
175 g/6 oz/¾ cup currants
175 g/6 oz/generous 1 cup raisins
75 g/3 oz/½ cup chopped mixed peel
150 g/5 oz/⅔ cup glacé (candied)
    cherries, halved
finely grated zest of 1 orange
30 ml/2 tbsp ground almonds
25 g/1 oz/¼ cup blanched
    almonds, chopped
120 ml/4 fl oz/½ cup milk
75 ml/5 tbsp sunflower oil
30 ml/2 tbsp malt vinegar
5 ml/1 tsp bicarbonate of soda (baking soda)

TO DECORATE
mixed nuts, such as pistachios, pecans and
    macadamias; glacé (candied) cherries
    and angelica
60 ml/4 tbsp clear honey, warmed

1 Preheat the oven to 150°C/300°F/ Gas 2. Grease a deep 20 cm/8 in square loose-based cake tin (pan), line with a double thickness of baking parchment and grease the paper.

2 Sift the flour and mixed spice into a large mixing bowl, adding the bran left in the sieve. Rub the butter into the flour until it resembles fine breadcrumbs. Stir in the sugar, dried fruits, peel, cherries, zest and almonds.

3 Warm 50 ml/2 fl oz/¼ cup of the milk in a pan, then add the sunflower oil and vinegar. Dissolve the bicarbonate of soda in the rest of the milk, then combine the two mixtures and stir into the dry ingredients.

4 Spoon the mixture into the tin and smooth the surface. Bake for about 2½ hours, or until a skewer inserted into the centre comes out clean. Leave in the tin for 5 minutes, then turn on to a wire rack, peel off the paper and leave to cool.

5 Place the mixed nuts, glacé cherries and angelica on top of the cake, then brush with the warmed honey.

Lemon Coconut Layer Cake

The tangy citrus flavour of lemon perfectly counterbalances the sweetness of the coconut in this rich cake.

Serves 8–10

INGREDIENTS
8 eggs
370 g/12¾ oz/scant 2 cups caster (superfine) sugar
15 ml/1 tbsp grated orange rind
grated rind of 2 lemons
juice of 1 lemon
65 g/2½ oz/¾ cup sweetened, shredded coconut
150 g/5 oz/1¼ cups plain (all-purpose) flour, sifted with 1.5 ml/¼ tsp salt
30 ml/2 tbsp cornflour (cornstarch)
250 ml/8 fl oz/1 cup water
75 g/3 oz/6 tbsp butter

FOR THE FROSTING
115 g/4 oz/½ cup unsalted (sweet) butter
115 g/4 oz/1 cup icing (confectioners') sugar
grated rind of 1 lemon
90–120 ml/6–8 tbsp lemon juice
115 g/4 oz/1⅓ cups sweetened shredded coconut

1 Preheat the oven to 180°C/350°F/ Gas 4. Line and grease three round 20 cm/8 in cake tins (pans) with a layer of baking parchment.

2 Place 6 of the eggs in a bowl set over hot water and beat until frothy. Beat in 165 g/5½ oz/¾ cup of the sugar until the mixture has doubled in volume.

3 Remove from the heat. Fold in the orange rind, half the lemon rind, 15 ml/1 tbsp of the lemon juice and the coconut. Sift over the flour mixture and fold in well.

4 Divide the mixture evenly between the three prepared cake tins. Bake for 25–30 minutes until the cakes start to pull away from the sides of the tins. Leave the cakes in the tins for 5 minutes, then transfer them to a wire rack to cool.

5 For the lemon custard, blend the cornflour with water. Whisk in the remaining eggs. Mix the remaining ingredients in a pan and bring to the boil. Add the cornflour and return to the boil. Whisk until thick. Remove and cover with clear film (plastic wrap).

6 For the frosting, cream the butter and icing sugar. Stir in the lemon rind and enough lemon juice to obtain a spreadable consistency. Sandwich the cake layers with the lemon custard. Spread the frosting over the top and sides. Cover with the coconut.

53

Apple Cake

Try this moist cake hot or cold.

Serves 8–10

INGREDIENTS
250 g/9 oz/2¼ cups self-raising (self-rising)
 flour
10 ml/2 tsp baking powder
5 ml/1 tsp ground cinnamon
130 g/4½ oz/generous ½ cup caster
 (superfine) sugar
50 g/2 oz/¼ cup butter, melted
2 eggs, beaten
150 ml/¼ pint/⅔ cup milk

FOR THE TOPPING
2 eating apples, peeled, cored and sliced
15 g/½ oz/1 tbsp butter, melted
60 ml/4 tbsp demerara (raw) sugar
1.5 ml/¼ tsp ground cinnamon

1 Preheat the oven to 200°C/400°F/
Gas 6. Grease and line a 20 cm/8 in
cake tin (pan). Sift the flour, baking
powder and cinnamon into a bowl.
Add the sugar. Whisk the butter, eggs
and milk, then stir these in too.

2 Pour the mixture into the tin, make
a shallow hollow around the edge, and
lay the apples around it. Brush with
the butter, then scatter with demerara
sugar and cinnamon.

3 Bake for 45–50 minutes, or until
a skewer inserted into the centre
comes out clean. Serve immediately or
cool on a wire rack.

Pear Cake

Polenta gives this a nutty flavour.

Serves 10

INGREDIENTS
175 g/6 oz/¾ cup golden caster
 (superfine) sugar
4 ripe pears, peeled, cored and sliced
juice of ½ lemon
30 ml/2 tbsp clear honey
3 eggs
seeds from 1 vanilla pod (bean)
120 ml/4 fl oz/½ cup sunflower oil
115 g/4 oz/1 cup self-raising
 (self-rising) flour
50 g/2 oz/½ cup instant polenta

1 Preheat the oven to 180°C/350°F/
Gas 4. Grease and line a 21 cm/
8½ in cake tin (pan). Scatter 30 ml/
2 tbsp sugar over the base of the tin.
Toss the pear slices in the lemon juice.
Arrange them on the base of the cake
tin. Drizzle the honey over the pears.

2 Beat together the eggs, vanilla pod
seeds and the remaining sugar in a
bowl until thick. Gradually beat in the
oil. Sift together the flour and polenta
and fold into the egg mixture.

3 Pour the mixture into the tin. Bake
for about 50 minutes, or until a skewer
inserted into the centre comes out
clean. Cool for 10 minutes, then peel
off the lining paper and slice.

Right: Apple Cake (top); Pear Cake

Greek Yogurt & Fig Cake

Baked fresh figs, thickly sliced, make a delectable base for a feather-light sponge. Firm figs work best for this recipe.

Serves 6–8

INGREDIENTS
6 firm fresh figs, thickly sliced
45 ml/3 tbsp clear honey, plus extra
   for glazing cooked figs
200 g/7 oz/scant 1 cup butter, softened
175 g/6 oz/scant 1 cup caster
   (superfine) sugar
grated rind of 1 lemon
grated rind of 1 orange
4 eggs, separated
225 g/8 oz/2 cups plain (all-purpose) flour
5 ml/1 tsp baking powder
5 ml/1 tsp bicarbonate of soda (baking soda)
250 ml/8 fl oz/1 cup Greek (US strained
   plain) yogurt

1 Preheat the oven to 180°C/350°F/Gas 4. Grease a 23 cm/9 in cake tin (pan) and line the base with non-stick baking parchment. Arrange the figs over the base of the tin and drizzle the honey over the top.

2 Cream the butter and caster sugar with the lemon and orange rinds until the mixture is pale and fluffy, then gradually beat in the egg yolks.

3 Sift the dry ingredients together. Add a little to the creamed mixture, beat well, then beat in a spoonful of yogurt. Repeat this process until all the dry ingredients and yogurt have been incorporated.

4 Whisk the egg whites until they form stiff peaks. Stir half the whites into the cake mixture to slacken it, then fold in the rest. Pour the mixture over the figs in the tin, then bake for 1¼ hours, or until a skewer inserted into the centre comes out clean.

5 Turn the cake out on to a wire rack, peel off the lining paper and cool. Drizzle the figs with extra honey before serving.

Upside-down Pear & Ginger Cake

A light, spicy sponge topped with glossy, baked fruit and ginger. This is also good served as a warm pudding, with cream or custard.

Serves 6–8

INGREDIENTS
900 g/2 lb can pear halves, drained
120 ml/8 tbsp finely chopped stem ginger
120 ml/8 tbsp ginger syrup from the jar
175 g/6 oz/1½ cups self-raising (self-rising) flour
2.5 ml/½ tsp baking powder
5 ml/1 tsp ground ginger
175 g/6 oz/¾ cup soft brown sugar
175 g/6 oz/¾ cup butter, softened
3 eggs, lightly beaten

1 Preheat the oven to 180°C/350°F/ Gas 4. Grease and line a deep 20 cm/ 8 in cake tin (pan).

2 Fill the hollow in each pear with half the chopped ginger. Arrange the pears, flat sides down, over the base of the cake tin, then spoon half the ginger syrup over the top.

3 Sift the flour, baking powder and ground ginger into a mixing bowl. Stir in the soft brown sugar and butter, then add the lightly beaten eggs and beat together for 1–2 minutes until the mixture is creamy.

4 Carefully spoon the mixture into the tin, spreading it out evenly so that all the pears are covered, and smooth the surface.

5 Bake for about 50 minutes, or until a skewer inserted into the centre comes out clean. Leave the cake to cool in the tin for about 5 minutes.

6 Turn out on to a wire rack, peel off the lining paper and leave to cool completely. Add the reserved chopped ginger to the pear halves on top of the cake and drizzle over the remaining ginger syrup.

Rich Chocolate Cake

This dark, fudgy cake is easy to make, stores well and is a chocolate lover's dream come true.

Serves 14–16

INGREDIENTS
250 g/9 oz plain (semisweet) chocolate,
  broken or chopped
225 g/8 oz/1 cup unsalted (sweet) butter,
  cut into pieces
5 eggs
90 g/3½ oz/½ cup caster (superfine)
  sugar, plus 15 ml/1 tbsp and extra
  for sprinkling
15 ml/1 tbsp unsweetened cocoa powder
10 ml/2 tsp vanilla essence (extract)
unsweetened cocoa powder, for dusting
chocolate shavings,
  to decorate

1 Preheat the oven to 160°C/325°F/ Gas 3. Lightly butter a 23 cm/9 in springform tin (pan) and line the base with non-stick baking parchment. Butter the parchment and sprinkle with a little sugar, then shake out the excess. Wrap a double thickness of foil around the outside of the base and sides of the tin.

2 Melt the chocolate and butter in a pan over a low heat, stirring frequently, until smooth, then remove from the heat.

3 Beat the eggs and the 90 g/3½ oz/ ½ cup of the sugar with an electric mixer for 1 minute.

4 Beat the cocoa and the remaining sugar into the egg mixture until well blended. Beat in the vanilla essence, then gradually beat in the melted chocolate until well blended. Pour the mixture into the prepared tin and tap gently to allow any air bubbles to rise to the surface.

5 Place the cake tin in a roasting pan and carefully pour in boiling water to come 2 cm/¾ in up the sides of the wrapped tin. Bake for 45–50 minutes, until the edge of the cake is set and the centre still soft.

6 Lift the tin out of the water and remove the foil wrapping. Place the cake, still in its tin, on a wire rack, remove the sides of the tin and leave it to cool completely (it will sink a little in the centre).

7 Invert the cake on to the wire rack. Remove the base of the tin and the paper. Dust the cake liberally with cocoa powder and arrange the chocolate shavings around the edge. Slide the cake on to a serving plate.

Summer Shortcake

A summertime treat. Don't add the cream and strawberries until just before serving, or the shortcakes will go soft.

Serves 8

INGREDIENTS

225 g/8 oz/2 cups plain (all-purpose) flour
15 ml/1 tbsp baking powder
2.5 ml/½ tsp salt
50 g/2 oz/4 tbsp caster (superfine) sugar
50 g/2 oz/4 tbsp butter, softened
150 ml/¼ pint/⅔ cup milk
300 ml/½ pint/1¼ cups double (heavy) cream
450 g/1 lb/4 cups fresh strawberries,
    halved and hulled

1 Preheat the oven to 220°C/425°F/ Gas 7. Grease a baking sheet, and line the base with baking parchment.

2 Sift the flour, baking powder and salt into a large mixing bowl. Stir in the sugar, cut in the butter and toss into the flour mixture with your fingers until it resembles coarse breadcrumbs. Stir in just enough milk to make a soft dough.

3 Turn out the dough on to a lightly floured work surface and, using your fingers, pat into a 30 x 15 cm/ 12 x 6 in rectangle. Using a template, cut out two 15 cm/6 in rounds, indent one dividing into eight portions, and place both on the baking sheet.

4 Bake in the centre of the oven for 10–15 minutes, or until slightly risen and golden. Leave on the baking sheet for about 5 minutes, then transfer to a wire rack, peel off the paper and let cool completely.

5 Place the cream in a mixing bowl and whip with an electric mixer until it holds soft peaks. Place the unmarked shortcake on a serving plate and spread or pipe with half the cream. Top with two-thirds of the strawberries, then the other shortcake. Decorate with the remaining cream and strawberries and serve chilled.

Frosted Chocolate Fudge Cake

Rich and dreamy, with an irresistible chocolate fudgy frosting, this cake couldn't be easier to make, or more wonderful to eat!

Serves 6–8

INGREDIENTS
115 g/4 oz plain (semisweet) chocolate, broken into squares
175 g/6 oz/¾ cup unsalted (sweet) butter or margarine, softened
200 g/7 oz/scant 1 cup light muscovado (brown) sugar
5 ml/1 tsp vanilla essence (extract)
3 eggs, beaten
150 ml/¼ pint/⅔ cup Greek (US strained plain) yogurt
150 g/5 oz/1¼ cups self-raising (self-rising) flour
chocolate curls, to decorate

FOR THE FROSTING
115 g/4 oz dark (bittersweet) chocolate
50 g/2 oz/4 tbsp unsalted (sweet) butter
350 g/12 oz/3 cups icing (confectioners') sugar
90 ml/6 tbsp Greek (US strained plain) yogurt

1 Preheat the oven to 190°C/375°F/ Gas 5. Grease two 20 cm/8 in round sandwich cake tins (pans) and line the base of each with a piece of non-stick baking parchment.

2 Break the plain chocolate into squares and place in a heatproof bowl over a pan of hot water.

3 In a mixing bowl, cream the butter or margarine with the sugar until light and fluffy. Beat in the vanilla essence, then gradually add the beaten eggs, beating well after each addition.

4 Stir in the melted chocolate and yogurt evenly. Fold in the flour using a metal spoon.

5 Divide the mixture between the tins. Bake for 25–30 minutes, or until firm to the touch. Turn out and cool on a wire rack.

6 Make the frosting. Melt the chocolate and butter in a pan over a low heat. Remove the pan from the heat and stir in the icing sugar and yogurt. Stir the mixture with a rubber spatula until it is smooth, then beat until the frosting begins to cool and thicken slightly. Use about a third of the mixture to sandwich the cooled cakes together.

7 Working quickly, spread the remaining frosting over the top. Decorate the cake with chocolate curls before serving.

COOK'S TIP: If the frosting begins to set too quickly, heat it gently to soften, and beat in a little extra yogurt if necessary.

Black Forest Gâteau

A rich, melt-in-the-mouth, layered gâteau that is ideal for serving as a sumptuous teatime treat.

Serves 10–12

INGREDIENTS
5 eggs
175 g/6 oz/scant 1 cup caster
   (superfine) sugar
50 g/2 oz/½ cup plain (all-purpose) flour
50 g/2 oz/½ cup unsweetened cocoa powder
75 g/3 oz/6 tbsp butter, melted

FOR THE FILLING
75–90 ml/5–6 tbsp kirsch
600 ml/1 pint/2½ cups double (heavy) cream
425 g/15 oz can black cherries, drained,
   pitted and chopped

TO DECORATE
chocolate curls
15–20 fresh cherries, preferably with stems
icing (confectioners') sugar

1 Preheat the oven to 180°C/350°F/ Gas 4. Base-line and grease two deep 20 cm/8 in round cake tins (pans).

2 Beat together the eggs and sugar for 10 minutes. Sift over the flour and cocoa, and fold in gently. Trickle in the melted butter and fold in gently.

3 Transfer to the cake tins. Bake for 30 minutes, or until springy. Leave in the tins for 5 minutes, then turn out on to a wire rack, peel off the paper and leave to cool.

4 Cut each cake in half horizontally and sprinkle each half with a quarter of the kirsch.

5 Whip the cream until softly peaking. Combine two-thirds of the cream with the chopped cherries. Place a layer of cake on a serving plate and spread with one-third of the filling. Repeat twice, and top with a layer of cake. Use the reserved cream to cover the top and sides.

6 Decorate the gâteau with chocolate curls and fresh cherries and dredge with icing sugar.

Tía Maria Gâteau

Whipped cream and Tía Maria make a mouth-watering filling for this light chocolate and walnut cake.

Serves 6–8

INGREDIENTS
150 g/5 oz/1¼ cups self-raising
   (self-rising) flour
25 g/1 oz/¼ cup unsweetened cocoa powder
7.5 ml/1½ tsp baking powder
3 eggs, beaten
175 g/6 oz/¾ cup butter, softened
175 g/6 oz/1 cup caster (superfine) sugar
50 g/2 oz/½ cup chopped walnuts
walnut brittle, to decorate

FOR THE FILLING AND COATING
600 ml/1 pint/2½ cups double (heavy) cream
45 ml/3 tbsp Tía Maria
50 g/2 oz/⅔ cup desiccated (dry unsweetened
   shredded) coconut, toasted

1 Preheat the oven to 160°C/325°F/ Gas 3. Grease and base-line two 18 cm/7 in sandwich tins (pans). Sift the flour, cocoa and baking powder into a large bowl.

2 Add the eggs, butter, sugar and walnuts and mix together. Divide between the cake tins, level the surface and bake for 35–40 minutes, until risen. Turn out and leave to cool.

3 For the filling add the Tía Maria to the cream and whisk until the mixture forms soft peaks.

4 Slice each cake horizontally in half to give four layers. Sandwich the layers together with some of the flavoured whipped cream.

COOK'S TIP: To make walnut brittle, melt 75 g/3 oz/6 tbsp caster (superfine) sugar in a pan. Stir in 50 g/2 oz/½ cup broken walnuts. Turn the mixture on to non-stick baking parchment and leave to set. Break the brittle into pieces with a rolling pin.

5 Coat the sides of the cake with cream, saving some for the top. Spread out the toasted coconut on a sheet of non-stick baking parchment. Then, holding the top and bottom of the cake, roll the sides in the coconut until evenly coated. Put the cake on a serving plate, spread more of the cream on top and pipe the remainder around the outside rim. Decorate inside the rim with walnut brittle.

White Chocolate Cappuccino Gâteau

Luscious, lavish and laced with liqueur, this magnificent gâteau is strictly for adults only!

Serves 8

INGREDIENTS
4 eggs
115 g/4 oz/generous ½ cup caster (superfine) sugar
15 ml/1 tbsp strong black coffee
2.5 ml/½ tsp vanilla essence (extract)
115 g/4 oz/1 cup plain (all-purpose) flour
75 g/3 oz white chocolate, coarsely grated

FOR THE FILLING
120 ml/4 fl oz/½ cup double (heavy) cream
15 ml/1 tbsp coffee liqueur

FOR THE FROSTING AND TOPPINGS
175 g/6 oz white chocolate broken into squares
75 g/3 oz/6 tbsp unsalted (sweet) butter
115 g/4 oz/1 cup icing (confectioners') sugar
90 ml/6 tbsp double (heavy) cream
15 ml/1 tbsp coffee liqueur
white chocolate curls
unsweetened cocoa powder, for dusting

1 Preheat the oven to 180°C/350°F/ Gas 4. Grease two deep 19 cm/7½ in round sandwich cake tins (pans) and line the base of each with non-stick baking parchment.

2 Whisk together the eggs, caster sugar, black coffee and vanilla essence in a bowl set over a pan of hot water, until the mixture is pale and thick enough to hold its shape when the whisk is lifted.

3 Sift half the flour over the mixture; fold in gently and evenly. Carefully fold in the remaining flour with the grated white chocolate.

4 Divide the mixture between the prepared tins and smooth. Bake for 20–25 minutes, until firm and golden brown, then turn out on wire racks and leave to cool completely.

5 Make the filling. Whip the cream with the coffee liqueur in a bowl until it holds its shape. Spread over one of the cakes, then place the second layer on top.

6 To make the frosting, melt the chocolate with the butter in a bowl set over hot water. Remove from the heat and beat in the icing sugar.

7 Whip the double cream until it just holds its shape, then beat into the chocolate mixture.

8 Allow the frosting to cool, stirring occasionally, until it begins to hold its shape. Stir the coffee liqueur into the frosting. Spread over the top and sides of the cake, swirling with a palette knife. Decorate the cake with curls of white chocolate and dust the top with cocoa powder.

Raspberry Meringue Gâteau

This rich meringue gâteau makes the most of wonderful fresh raspberries when they are in season.

Serves 6

INGREDIENTS
4 egg whites
225 g/8 oz/generous 1 cup caster
    (superfine) sugar
few drops vanilla essence (extract)
5 ml/1 tsp distilled malt vinegar
115 g/4 oz/1 cup roasted and chopped
    hazelnuts, ground
300 ml/½ pint/1¼ cups double
    (heavy) cream
350 g/12 oz/2 cups raspberries
icing (confectioners') sugar, for dusting
mint sprigs, to decorate

FOR THE SAUCE
225 g/8 oz/1⅓ cups raspberries
45–60 ml/3–4 tbsp icing (confectioners')
    sugar, sifted
15 ml/1 tbsp orange liqueur

1 Preheat the oven to 180°C/350°F/
Gas 4. Grease and base-line two
20 cm/8 in sandwich tins (pans).

2 Whisk the egg whites until they
hold stiff peaks, then whisk in the
caster sugar a tablespoon at a time,
whisking well after each addition.

3 Continue whisking the meringue
mixture for 1–2 minutes, until very
stiff, then fold in the vanilla essence,
vinegar and ground hazelnuts.

4 Divide the mixture between the
sandwich tins and spread level. Bake
for 50–60 minutes, until crisp. Remove
from the tins and leave to cool on a
wire rack.

5 To make the sauce, process the
raspberries with the icing sugar and
liqueur in a blender or food processor,
then press the purée through a fine
sieve to remove any pips (seeds). Chill
until ready to serve.

6 Whip the cream until it forms soft peaks, then fold in the raspberries. Sandwich the meringue rounds together with the raspberry cream.

7 Dust the top of the gâteau with icing sugar. Decorate with mint sprigs and serve with the raspberry sauce.

Apricot Brandy-snap Roulade

A magnificent combination of soft and crisp textures, this cake looks impressive and is easy to prepare.

Serves 6–8

INGREDIENTS
4 eggs, separated
7.5 ml/1½ tsp fresh orange juice
115 g/4 oz/½ cup caster (superfine) sugar
175 g/6 oz/1½ cups ground almonds
4 brandy-snaps, crushed, to decorate

FOR THE FILLING
150 g/5 oz canned apricots, drained
300 ml/½ pint/1¼ cups double (heavy) cream
25 g/1 oz/4 tbsp icing (confectioners') sugar

1 Preheat the oven to 190°C/375°F/Gas 5. Grease a 33 x 23 cm/13 x 9 in Swiss roll tin (jelly roll pan), line the base of the tin with baking parchment and grease the paper.

2 Beat the egg yolks, orange juice and sugar with an electric mixer for about 10 minutes, until thick and pale. Fold in the ground almonds.

3 Whisk the egg whites until they hold stiff peaks. Fold them into the almond mixture, then transfer to the tin and smooth the surface.

4 Bake for about 20 minutes, or until a skewer inserted into the centre of the cake comes out clean. Leave the cake to cool in the tin, covered with a clean, just-damp cloth.

5 To make the filling, process the drained apricots in a blender or food processor until they reach a smooth consistency. Whip the cream and icing sugar until the cream holds soft peaks. Fold the apricot purée into the cream and icing sugar mixture.

6 Spread out the crushed brandy-snaps on a sheet of baking parchment. Spread about one-third of the cream mixture over the cooled cake, then invert it on to the layer of crushed brandy-snaps. Peel away the lining paper from the cake.

7 Cover the cake with the remaining cream mixture, then, using the baking parchment as a guide, roll up the roulade from a short end. Transfer to a serving dish with the join underneath, sticking on any extra pieces of crushed brandy-snaps.

Pineapple & Kirsch Gâteaux

A dramatic effect is created when this cake, with its kirsch-flavoured creamy filling, is sliced to reveal the striped pattern inside.

Serves 10–12

INGREDIENTS
175 g/6 oz/¾ cup butter
115 g/4 oz/½ cup caster (superfine) sugar, plus extra for sprinkling
2 eggs, lightly beaten
115 g/4 oz/1 cup self-raising (self-rising) flour, sifted
10 ml/2 tsp grated lemon rind
225 g/8 oz ginger nut biscuits (gingersnaps)
pineapple wedges and leaves, to decorate

FOR THE FILLING AND COATING
750 ml/1¼ pints/3 cups double (heavy) cream
30 ml/2 tbsp kirsch
225 g/8 oz fresh pineapple, finely chopped
115 g/4 oz/1⅓ cups desiccated (dry unsweetened shredded) coconut, toasted

1 Preheat the oven to 200°C/400°F/ Gas 6. Grease and line a 28 x 18 cm/ 11 x 7 in Swiss roll tin (jelly roll pan). and a 20 cm/8 in round springform cake tin (pan). Put 50 g/2 oz/4 tbsp of the butter, the sugar, eggs, flour and lemon rind in a bowl and beat until light and fluffy. Spread the mixture in the Swiss roll tin and bake for 10–12 minutes, until firm and golden.

2 Meanwhile, melt the remaining butter in a pan, crush the biscuits and stir in. Press the crumb mixture over the base of the round cake tin.

3 When the cake is cooked, turn it out on to a sheet of non-stick baking parchment sprinkled with caster sugar. Remove the lining paper.

4 Make the filling and coating. Whip the cream and combine half of it with the kirsch and the chopped pineapple. Spread the mixture over the cake and then cut the cake into four long strips.

5 Roll up the first strip of cake and filling and stand it on one end in the tin on the biscuit base. Wrap the remaining strips around to form a 20 cm/8 in cake. Chill for 15 minutes.

6 Carefully remove the cake from the tin and place it on a serving plate. Spoon some of the remaining cream into a piping bag and spread the rest over top and side of the cake. Cover with toasted coconut. Pipe swirls of cream on top of the cake and decorate with pineapple wedges and leaves.

COOK'S TIP: Give a marbled effect to the cake by colouring half the sponge mixture with a few drops of food colouring. Put alternate spoonfuls of plain and tinted into the tin and swirl with a skewer before baking.

Caramel Meringue Gâteau with Sloe Gin

Two crisp rounds of orange meringue are filled with a refreshing blend of cream, mango, grapes and sloe gin.

Serves 8

INGREDIENTS
4 egg whites
225 g/8 oz/1 cup soft light
    brown sugar
3 drops of white wine vinegar
3 drops of vanilla essence (extract)
10 ml/2 tsp grated orange rind
whipped cream, to decorate

FOR THE FILLING AND
    CARAMEL TOPPING
300 ml/½ pint/1¼ cups double
    (heavy) cream
45 ml/3 tbsp sloe gin
1 mango, chopped
225 g/8 oz mixed green and black
    seedless grapes, halved
75 g/3 oz/6 tbsp granulated sugar

3 Make the filling. Whip the double cream in a large bowl until it is fairly thick, then carefully fold in the sloe gin, chopped mango and halved green and black grapes using a wooden spoon.

1 Preheat the oven to 160°C/325°F/ Gas 3. Base-line two 20 cm/8 in sandwich tins (pans). Whisk the egg whites until stiff. Add half the sugar and continue to whisk until the meringue softens again.

2 Fold in the remaining sugar, the white wine vinegar, vanilla essence and grated orange rind. Divide the mixture between the tins, spread evenly and bake for 40 minutes. Leave to cool.

4 Gently spread one meringue layer with the whipped cream and fruit mixture, then place the second meringue layer on top of the filling and press it down firmly but carefully, so that the delicate meringue does not break. Transfer the gâteau to a serving plate.

5 Line a baking sheet with baking parchment. Put the sugar for the caramel topping into a heavy pan. Heat gently until it melts. Increase the heat and cook, without stirring, until it becomes golden and a spoonful hardens when dropped into cold water.

6 Drizzle some of the caramel on to the baking parchment to make decorative shapes and allow these to cool and harden. Drizzle the remaining caramel over the gâteau. Decorate the top with the whipped cream and stand the cooled caramel shapes upright in the cream.

COOKIES

Ladies' Kisses

These old-fashioned Italian cookies are just the thing for a special tea party.

Makes 20

INGREDIENTS
150 g/5 oz/10 tbsp butter, softened
115 g/4 oz/½ cup caster (superfine) sugar
1 egg yolk
2.5 ml/½ tsp almond essence (extract)
115 g/4 oz/1 cup ground almonds
175 g/6 oz/1½ cups plain (all-purpose) flour
50 g/2 oz plain (semi-sweet) chocolate

1 Cream the butter and sugar together with an electric mixer until light and fluffy, then beat in the yolk, almond essence, almonds and flour until evenly mixed. Chill until firm.

2 Preheat the oven to 160°C/325°F/Gas 3. Line three to four baking sheets with non-stick baking parchment. Break off small pieces of dough and roll into 40 balls. Place well apart on the baking sheets.

3 Bake for 20 minutes, or until golden. Remove the baking sheets from the oven, lift off the paper with the biscuits on, then place on wire racks to cool.

4 Lift the cold cookies off the paper. Melt the chocolate and use it to sandwich the biscuits in pairs. Leave to cool and set before serving.

Tea Cookies

If you don't want to pipe the mixture, spoon it on to the baking sheets and press with a fork.

Makes 20

INGREDIENTS
150 g/5 oz/10 tbsp butter, softened
75 g/3 oz/¾ cup icing (confectioners') sugar, sifted
1 egg, beaten
a few drops of almond essence (extract)
225 g/8 oz/2 cups plain (all-purpose) flour
2–3 large pieces of candied peel

1 Preheat the oven to 230°C/450°F/Gas 8. Line two baking sheets with non-stick baking paper. Cream the butter and sugar with an electric mixer until light and fluffy, then beat in the egg, almond essence and flour until evenly mixed.

2 Spoon the mixture into a piping bag fitted with a star nozzle and pipe 10 rosette shapes on each of the baking sheets.

3 Cut the candied peel into small diamond shapes and press one diamond into the centre of each cookie. Bake for 5 minutes, or until golden. Transfer the cookies on the baking sheet to a wire rack to cool completely. Lift the cookies off the paper when cool.

Right: Ladies' Kisses (top); Tea Cookies

Mocha Viennese Swirls

Some temptations just can't be resisted. Put out a plate of these melt-in-the-mouth marvels and watch them vanish.

Makes about 20

INGREDIENTS
200 g/7 oz/scant 1 cup unsalted (sweet)
   butter, softened, plus extra for greasing
50 g/2 oz/½ cup icing (confectioners') sugar
115 g/4 oz plain (semisweet) chocolate
30 ml/2 tbsp strong black coffee
200 g/7 oz/scant 2 cups plain
   (all-purpose) flour
50 g/2 oz/½ cup cornflour (cornstarch)

FOR THE DECORATION
about 20 blanched almonds
150 g/5 oz plain (semisweet) chocolate

2 Spoon the mixture into a piping bag fitted with a large star nozzle and pipe about 20 swirls on the baking sheets, allowing room for spreading during baking.

3 Press an almond into the centre of each swirl. Bake for about 15 minutes, or until the biscuits are firm and just beginning to brown. Leave to cool for about 10 minutes on the baking sheets, then transfer to a wire rack to cool completely.

4 When cold, melt the plain chocolate for the decoration, and dip the base of each swirl to coat. Place the coated biscuits on a sheet of non-stick baking paper and leave to set.

1 Preheat the oven to 190°C/375°F/Gas 5. Lightly grease two large baking sheets. Break the chocolate into squares and melt in a bowl over hot water. Cream the butter with the icing sugar in a bowl until smooth and pale. Beat in the melted chocolate, then the coffee. Sift the plain flour and cornflour over the mixture. Fold in lightly to make a soft mixture.

COOK'S TIP: If the mixture is too stiff to pipe, soften it with a little more black coffee.

Vanilla Crescents

These attractive little almond and vanilla-flavoured biscuits are
absolutely irresistible.

Makes 36

INGREDIENTS
175 g/6 oz/1 cup unblanched almonds
115 g/4 oz/1 cup plain (all-purpose) flour
2.5 ml/½ tsp salt
225 g/8 oz/1 cup butter, at room temperature,
    plus extra for greasing
90 g/3½ oz/½ cup sugar
5 ml/1 tsp vanilla essence (extract)
icing (confectioners') sugar, for dusting

1 Put the almonds and a few
tablespoons of the flour in a food
processor or blender, and process.

2 Sift the remaining flour with the
salt. Set aside. With an electric mixer,
cream the butter and sugar together
in a bowl until light and fluffy.

3 Add the almonds, vanilla essence
and the flour mixture. Stir to mix well.
Gather the dough into a ball, wrap in
baking parchment and chill in the
refrigerator for at least 30 minutes.

4 Preheat the oven to 160°C/325°F/
Gas 3. Lightly grease two baking
sheets. Break off walnut-size pieces of
dough and roll into small cylinders
about 1 cm/½ in diameter. Bend into
small crescents and place on the
prepared baking sheets.

5 Bake for about 20 minutes, until
dry but not brown. Transfer to a rack
to cool slightly. Set the rack over a
baking sheet and dust with an even
layer of icing sugar.

COOK'S TIPS: Chilling the dough
makes it firmer and therefore easier
to shape.
    Bake cookies at or just above the
centre of the oven. If you are using
two baking sheets, place one above
the other and swap them over
halfway through the cooking time,
so that they brown evenly.

Chocolate Chip Cookies

Keep a supply of these favourite cookies stored in the freezer.

Makes 16

INGREDIENTS
75 g/3 oz/6 tbsp soft margarine, plus extra
    for greasing
50 g/2 oz/¼ cup soft light brown sugar
50 g/2 oz/¼ cup caster (superfine) sugar
1 egg, beaten
few drops of vanilla essence (extract)
75 g/3 oz/¾ cup rice flour
75 g/3 oz/¾ cup cornmeal
5 ml/1 tsp baking powder
115 g/4 oz/⅔ cup plain (semisweet) chocolate
    chips, or a mixture of milk and white
    chocolate chips
salt

1 Preheat the oven to 190°C/375°F/
Gas 5. Lightly grease two baking
sheets. Cream the margarine and
sugars together until light and fluffy.

2 Beat in the egg and vanilla essence.
Fold in the rice flour, cornmeal,
baking powder and a pinch of salt,
then fold in the chocolate chips.

3 Place spoonfuls of the mixture on
the baking sheets, spaced well apart.
Bake for 10–15 minutes, until the
cookies are lightly browned. Leave on
the baking sheets for a few minutes,
then cool on a wire rack.

Cherry Munchies

You'll find it hard to stop at just one of these munchies.

Makes 20

INGREDIENTS
2 egg whites
115 g/4 oz/1 cup icing (confectioners')
    sugar, sifted
115 g/4 oz/1 cup ground almonds
115 g/4 oz/generous 1 cup desiccated (dry
    unsweetened shredded) coconut
few drops of almond essence (extract)
75 g/3 oz/½ cup glacé (candied) cherries,
    finely chopped

1 Preheat the oven to 150°C/300°F/
Gas 2. Line two baking sheets with
non-stick baking paper. Place the egg
whites in a bowl and whisk until stiff.

2 Fold in the icing sugar, then fold in
the ground almonds, coconut and
almond essence to form a sticky
dough. Fold in the chopped cherries.

3 Place heaped teaspoonfuls of the
mixture on the prepared baking sheets.
Bake for 25 minutes, or until pale
golden. Cool on the baking sheets for
a few minutes, then transfer to a wire
rack until cold.

Right: Chocolate Chip Cookies (top);
Cherry Munchies

Lavender Heart Cookies

Serve these fragrant cookies on any romantic anniversary.

Makes 16–18

INGREDIENTS

115 g/4 oz/½ cup unsalted (sweet) butter
90 ml/6 tbsp caster (superfine) sugar
175 g/6 oz/1½ cups plain (all-purpose) flour,
  plus extra for dusting
30 ml/2 tbsp fresh lavender florets
  or 15 ml/1 tbsp dried culinary lavender,
  roughly chopped

1 Cream the butter and 60 ml/4 tbsp of sugar together until fluffy. Stir in the flour and lavender and bring the mixture together in a soft ball. Cover and chill for 15 minutes.

2 Preheat the oven to 200°C/400°F/ Gas 6. Roll out the dough on a lightly floured surface and stamp out about 18 cookies, using a 5 cm/2 in heart-shaped cutter. Place on a heavy baking sheet and bake for about 10 minutes, or until golden.

3 Leave the cookies standing for 5 minutes, then transfer them carefully to a wire rack to cool.

COOK'S TIP: These cookies would make an unusual gift, contained in an airtight jar decorated with ribbon.

Chocolate Crackle-tops

Makes about 38 cookies

INGREDIENTS

200 g/7 oz dark (bittersweet) or plain
  (semisweet) chocolate, chopped
90 g/3½ oz/7 tbsp unsalted (sweet) butter,
  plus extra for greasing
115 g/4 oz/⅔ cup caster (superfine) sugar
3 eggs
5 ml/1 tsp vanilla essence (extract)
215 g/7½ oz/2 cups plain (all-purpose) flour
25 g/1 oz/¼ cup unsweetened cocoa powder
2.5 ml/½ tsp baking powder
pinch of salt
175 g/6 oz/1½ cups icing (confectioners')
  sugar

1 Melt the chocolate and butter in a pan over low heat, stirring frequently. Remove from heat. Add the sugar, stirring for 2–3 minutes until dissolved. Add the eggs, one at a time, beating after each addition. Stir in the vanilla.

2 Sift the flour, cocoa, baking powder and salt into a bowl. Gradually stir into the chocolate mixture until blended. Cover and chill for at least 1 hour.

3 Preheat the oven to 160°C/325°F/ Gas 3. Grease two baking sheets. Place the icing sugar in a small bowl. Take teaspoonfuls of dough and roll into 4 cm/1½ in balls.

4 Drop the balls, one at a time, into the icing sugar and roll until heavily coated. Remove with a slotted spoon and tap against the side of the bowl to remove any excess sugar. Place on baking sheets 4 cm/1½ in apart.

5 Bake the cookies for 10–15 minutes, or until slightly firm when touched. Leave on the baking sheet for 2–3 minutes to set then cool on a wire rack.

Coffee Sponge Drops

Low-fat cheese and stem ginger make a delicious filling for these lovely
light sponge drops.

Makes 12

INGREDIENTS
50 g/2 oz/½ cup plain (all-purpose) flour
15 ml/1 tbsp instant coffee powder
2 eggs
75 g/3 oz/scant ½ cup caster
  (superfine) sugar

FOR THE FILLING
115 g/4 oz/¼ cup low-fat soft cheese
40 g/1½ oz/¼ cup chopped stem ginger

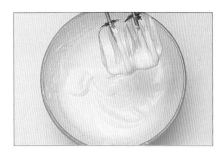

2 Combine the eggs and caster sugar
in a bowl. Beat with a hand-held
electric whisk until thick and mousse-
like (when the whisk is lifted a trail
should remain on the surface of the
mixture for at least 15 seconds).

1 Preheat the oven to 190°C/375°F/
Gas 5. Line two baking sheets with
non-stick baking parchment. Make the
filling by beating together the soft
cheese and stem ginger. Chill until
required. Sift the flour and instant
coffee powder together.

VARIATION: If liked, use the rind
of one orange in place of the stem
ginger and add 15 ml/1 tbsp
caster (superfine) sugar.

3 Carefully add the sifted flour and
coffee mixture and gently fold in with
a metal spoon.

4 Spoon the mixture into a piping
(pastry) bag fitted with a 1 cm/½ in
plain nozzle. Pipe 4 cm/1½ in rounds
on the baking sheets. Bake for 12
minutes. Cool on a wire rack.
Sandwich together with the filling.

Flapjacks

Low in fat and sugar, high in crunch factor and flavour – what better for teatime?

Makes 16

INGREDIENTS
oil, for brushing
115 g/4 oz/½ cup low-fat spread
60 ml/4 tbsp rice syrup
50 g/2 oz/½ cup wholemeal
    (whole-wheat) flour
225 g/8 oz/generous 2 cups rolled oats
50 g/2 oz/⅓ cup pine nuts

1 Preheat the oven to 180°C/350°F/ Gas 4. Line a 20 cm/8 in shallow baking tin (pan) with oiled foil. Melt the low-fat spread and rice syrup in a small pan over a low heat, then stir in the flour, oats and pine nuts until well mixed.

2 Turn the mixture into the tin and pat it out evenly with your fingers. Press the mixture down lightly. Bake for 25–30 minutes, until the flapjacks are lightly browned and crisp. Mark into squares while still warm. Cool slightly, then transfer to a wire rack.

COOK'S TIP: Do not let the syrup mixture boil or the flapjacks will be tacky rather than crisp.

Right: Flapjacks (top); Ginger Figures

Ginger Figures

Surprisingly, each of these charming, plump little figures contains less than 2 grams of fat.

Makes 8

INGREDIENTS
115 g/4 oz/1 cup plain (all-purpose) flour,
    sifted, plus extra for dusting
7.5 ml/1½ tsp ground ginger
grated rind of 1 orange and 1 lemon
75 ml/5 tbsp pear and apple spread or
    maple syrup
25 g/1 oz/ 2 tbsp low-fat spread
16 currants and 8 raisins, to decorate

1 Preheat the oven to 180°C/350°F/ Gas 4. Mix the flour, ginger and grated orange and lemon rind in a bowl. Melt the pear and apple spread and the low-fat spread in a pan over a low heat.

2 As soon as the pear and apple spread mixture has melted, stir it into the dry ingredients. Mix to a firm dough in the bowl, then wrap the dough in clear film (plastic wrap) and chill for 2–3 hours.

3 Roll out the dough on a lightly floured surface to a thickness of about 5 mm/¼ in. Cut out figures, using a cutter or a template.

4 Use currants for eyes and raisins for noses. Draw a mouth using the point of a knife. Place the figures on a lightly floured baking sheet and bake for 8–10 minutes. Cool on a wire rack.

Almond Tuiles

These cookies are named after the French roof tiles they resemble. Making them is a little fiddly, so bake only four at a time until you get the knack.

Makes about 24

INGREDIENTS
40 g/1½ oz/3 tbsp unsalted (sweet) butter,
  plus extra for greasing
65 g/2½ oz/½ cup whole blanched almonds,
  lightly toasted
65 g/2½ oz/⅓ cup caster (superfine) sugar
2 egg whites
2.5 ml/½ tsp almond essence (extract)
35 g/1¼ oz/scant ⅓ cup plain (all-purpose)
  flour, sifted
50 g/2 oz/½ cup flaked (sliced) almonds

1 Preheat the oven to 200°C/400°F/ Gas 6. Butter two heavy baking sheets.

2 Place the almonds and 30 ml/2 tbsp of the sugar in a food processor and pulse until finely ground, but not pasty.

3 With an electric mixer, beat the butter until creamy, then add the remaining caster sugar and beat for 12 minutes, until light and fluffy. Gradually beat in the egg whites, then beat in the almond essence. Sift the flour over the mixture and fold in, then fold in the ground almond mixture.

> COOK'S TIP: If the cookies flatten or go soft, reheat them on a baking sheet at 180°C/350°F/Gas 4, until completely flat, then reshape.

4 Drop tablespoons of mixture on to the baking sheets about 15 cm/6 in apart. With the back of a wet spoon, spread each mound into a paper-thin 7.5 cm/3 in round. (Don't worry if holes appear, they will fill in.) Sprinkle each round with a few flaked almonds.

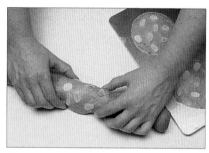

5 Bake the cookies, one sheet at a time, for 5–6 minutes, or until the edges are golden and the centres still pale. Remove the baking sheet to a wire rack and, working quickly, use a thin metal spatula to loosen the edges of one cookie. Carefully place the cookie over a rolling pin, then press down the sides of the cookie to curve it.

6 Continue shaping the cookies, transferring them to a wire rack as they cool and crisp. If the cookies become too crisp to shape, return the baking sheet to the hot oven for 15–30 seconds to soften them, then continue as before.

VARIATION: A few chopped glacé (candied) fruits could be sprinkled over the top of the cookies with the almonds, if liked.

Gingersnaps

Crisp and crunchy, gingersnaps are firm favourites with all the family.

Makes 60

INGREDIENTS
115 g/4 oz/½ cup butter, at room
    temperature, plus extra for greasing
275 g/10 oz/2½ cups plain (all-purpose) flour
5 ml/1 tsp bicarbonate of soda (baking soda)
7.5 ml/1½ tsp ground ginger
1.5 ml/¼ tsp ground cinnamon
1.5 ml/¼ tsp ground cloves
300 g/11 oz/generous 1½ cups sugar
1 egg, lightly beaten
60 ml/4 tbsp molasses or black treacle
5 ml/1 tsp lemon juice

1 Preheat the oven to 180°C/350°F/
Gas 4. Grease four baking sheets. Sift
the flour, bicarbonate of soda and
spices into a bowl. Set aside.

2 With an electric mixer, cream the
butter and 200 g/7 oz/1 cup of the
sugar together. Stir in the egg, molasses
or treacle and lemon juice. Add the
flour mixture and mix thoroughly with
a wooden spoon to make a soft dough.

3 Shape into 2 cm/¾ in balls. Roll
in the remaining sugar and place
5 cm/2 in apart on the baking sheets.
Bake for 12 minutes, or until just firm.
Leave to cool for a few minutes, then
transfer to a wire rack.

Right: Gingersnaps (top); Cowboy Bakes

Cowboy Bakes

There'll be no need to corral the kids at teatime for these tasty treats.

Makes 60

INGREDIENTS
115 g/4 oz/½ cup butter, plus extra
    for greasing
115 g/4 oz/1 cup plain (all-purpose) flour
2.5 ml/½ tsp bicarbonate of soda
    (baking soda)
1.5 ml/¼ tsp baking powder
1.5 ml/¼ tsp salt
90 g/3½ oz/½ cup granulated sugar
115 g/4 oz/½ cup brown sugar
1 egg
2.5 ml/½ tsp vanilla essence (extract)
90 g/3½ oz/1 cup rolled oats
175 g/6 oz/1 cup milk chocolate chips

1 Preheat the oven to 160°C/325°F/
Gas 3. Grease three or four baking
sheets. Sift the flour, bicarbonate of
soda, baking powder and salt into a
mixing bowl. Set aside.

2 With an electric mixer, cream the
butter and sugars together. Add the egg
and vanilla and beat until light and
fluffy. Add the flour mixture and beat
on low speed until blended. Stir in the
oats and chocolate, mixing well. The
dough should be crumbly.

3 Drop heaped teaspoons on to the
baking sheets, 2.5 cm/1 in apart. Bake
for 15 minutes, or until just firm
around the edge. Cool on a wire rack.

Apricot Yogurt Cookies

You can afford to indulge yourself with these low-fat, low-cholesterol, flavour-packed fruity cookies.

Makes 16

INGREDIENTS
45 ml/3 tbsp sunflower oil, plus extra
    for brushing
175 g/6 oz/1½ cups plain (all-purpose) flour
5 ml/1 tsp baking powder
5 ml/1 tsp ground cinnamon
75 g/3 oz/scant 1 cup rolled oats
75 g/3 oz/scant ½ cup light muscovado
    (brown) sugar
115 g/4 oz/½ cup chopped ready-to-eat
    dried apricots
15 ml/1 tbsp flaked (sliced) almonds or
    chopped hazelnuts
150 ml/¼ pint/⅔ cup natural (plain) yogurt
demerara (raw) sugar,
    for sprinkling

2 Beat together the yogurt and oil, then stir evenly into the mixture to make a firm dough. If necessary, add a little more yogurt.

3 Use your hands to roll the mixture into about 16 small balls, place on the baking sheet and flatten with a fork. Sprinkle with demerara sugar.

1 Preheat the oven to 190°C/375°F/ Gas 5. Lightly oil a large baking sheet. Stir together the flour, baking powder and cinnamon. Stir in the oats, sugar, apricots and nuts.

VARIATIONS: If liked, use unsulphured dried apricots, as these have a richer flavour. Dried dates could replace the apricots.

4 Bake for 15–20 minutes, or until firm and golden brown. Transfer to a wire rack to cool.

COOK'S TIP: These cookies do not keep well, so it is best to eat them within two days, or to freeze them. Pack into a plastic bag and freeze for up to four months.

Sultana Cookies

Makes about 48

INGREDIENTS
75 g/3 oz/½ cup sultanas (golden raisins)
225 g/8 oz/1 cup butter, plus extra
  for greasing
115 g/4 oz/1 cup finely ground
  yellow cornmeal
175 g/6 oz/1½ cups plain (all-purpose) flour
7.5 ml/1½ tsp baking powder
2.5 ml/½ tsp salt
225 g/8 oz/generous 1 cup
  granulated sugar
2 eggs
15 ml/1 tbsp Marsala or 5 ml/1 tsp vanilla
  essence (extract)

1 Soak the sultanas in a small bowl
of warm water for 15 minutes. Drain.
Preheat the oven to 180°C/350°F/
Gas 4. Grease two baking sheets.

2 Sift the cornmeal, flour, baking
powder and salt into a bowl. Cream
the butter and sugar together until
light and fluffy. Beat in the eggs, one at
a time. Beat in the Marsala or vanilla
essence. Add the dry ingredients to the
batter, beating until well blended. Stir
in the sultanas.

3 Drop heaped teaspoons of batter
on to the baking sheets in rows about
5 cm/2 in apart. Bake for 7–8 minutes,
or until golden brown at the edges.
Transfer to a wire rack to cool.

Right: Sultana Cookies (top); Amaretti

Amaretti

Makes about 36

INGREDIENTS
200 g/7 oz/1¼ cups blanched almonds
225 g/8 oz/generous 1 cup caster
  (superfine) sugar
2 egg whites
2.5 ml/½ tsp almond essence (extract)
flour, for dusting
icing (confectioners') sugar, for dusting

1 Preheat the oven to 160°C/325°F/
Gas 3. Spread out the almonds on a
baking sheet and place in the oven for
10–15 minutes without browning.
Remove from the oven and allow to
cool. Turn the oven off. Finely grind
the almonds with half the sugar in a
food processor.

2 Beat the egg whites until they form
soft peaks. Sprinkle half the remaining
sugar over them and continue beating.
Fold in the remaining sugar, the
almond essence and almonds.

3 Spoon the mixture into a pastry
bag with a smooth nozzle. Line a
baking sheet with baking parchment.
Dust with flour. Pipe the mixture in
walnut-size rounds. Sprinkle with
icing sugar and set aside for about
2 hours. Preheat the oven to 180°C/
350°F/Gas 4.

4 Bake for 15 minutes, or until pale
gold. Cool on a wire rack.

Glazed Gingerbread Cookies

Look for interesting-shaped cutters to make these cookies special.

Makes about 20

INGREDIENTS
175 g/6 oz/1½ cups plain (all-purpose) flour,
 plus extra for dusting
1.5 ml/¼ tsp bicarbonate of soda
 (baking soda)
5 ml/1 tsp ground ginger
5 ml/1 tsp ground cinnamon
65 g/2½ oz/5 tbsp unsalted (sweet) butter, cut
 into pieces, plus extra for greasing
75 g/3 oz/scant ½ cup caster (superfine) sugar
30 ml/2 tbsp maple syrup
1 egg yolk, beaten
red and green food colouring
175 g/6 oz white marzipan
salt

FOR THE ICING GLAZE
30 ml/2 tbsp lightly beaten egg white
30 ml/2 tbsp lemon juice
175–225 g/6–8 oz/1½–2 cups icing
 (confectioners') sugar

1 Sift together the flour, bicarbonate of soda, spices and a pinch of salt into a large bowl. Rub in the butter. Add the sugar, syrup and egg yolk and mix to a firm dough. Knead lightly, wrap and chill for 30 minutes.

2 Preheat the oven to 180°C/350°F/ Gas 4. Grease a large baking sheet. Roll out the dough on a floured surface and stamp out decorative shapes with novelty cookie cutters.

3 Transfer to the prepared sheet and bake for 8–10 minutes, until the cookies are beginning to colour around the edges. Leave on the baking sheet for 2 minutes until the cookies begin to harden, then transfer to a wire rack to cool.

4 To make the glaze, mix the egg white and lemon juice in a bowl. Gradually beat in the icing sugar until the mixture is smooth and has the consistency of thin cream. Place the wire rack over a tray or plate. Spoon the icing glaze over the cookies until they are completely covered. Leave in a cool place to dry for several hours.

5 Knead red food colouring into half the marzipan and green into the other half. Roll a thin length of each piece and then twist together into a rope. Secure a rope of marzipan around a cookie, dampening the icing with a little water, if necessary, to hold the marzipan twist in place. Repeat on about half the cookies.

6 Dilute a little of each food colouring with water. Using a fine brush, paint decorations on the plain cookies. Leave to dry.

COOK'S TIP: These biscuits can be made to suit the occasion, such as Christmas, as here, or birthdays.

Christmas Cookies

These festive cookies would make a lovely present – as well as a special teatime treat on Christmas day.

Makes about 12

INGREDIENTS
75 g/3 oz/6 tbsp butter, plus extra
    for greasing
50 g/2 oz/½ cup icing (confectioners') sugar
finely grated rind of 1 small lemon
1 egg yolk
175 g/6 oz/1½ cups plain (all-purpose) flour,
    plus extra for dusting
salt

TO DECORATE
2 egg yolks
red and green food colouring

1 In a large bowl, beat the butter, sugar and lemon rind together until pale and fluffy. Beat in the egg yolk, and then sift in the flour and a pinch of salt. Knead together to form a smooth dough. Wrap in clear film (plastic wrap) and chill for 30 minutes.

2 Preheat the oven to190°C/375°F/Gas 5. Lightly grease two baking sheets. On a lightly floured surface, roll out the dough to 3 mm/⅛ in thick.

3 Using a 6 cm/2½ in fluted cutter, stamp out as many cookies as you can, with the cutter dipped in flour to prevent it from sticking to the dough. Transfer the cookies to the prepared sheets.

4 For the decoration, mark the cookies lightly with a 2.5 cm/1 in holly leaf cutter and use a 5 mm/¼ in plain piping (icing) nozzle for the berries. Chill for 10 minutes.

5 Put each egg yolk for the decoration into a small cup. Mix red food colouring into one and green food colouring into the other. Using a small brush, paint the colours on to the cookies. Bake for 10–12 minutes, or until they begin to colour around the edges. Cool slightly on the baking sheets, then transfer to a wire rack.

Mini Florentines with Grand Marnier

Orange liqueur adds a luxury note to these ever-popular nut and dried fruit cookies. The are just as good made with raisins or walnuts.

Makes about 24

INGREDIENTS
50 g/2 oz/¼ cup soft light brown sugar
15 ml/1 tbsp clear honey
15 ml/1 tbsp Grand Marnier
50 g/2 oz/¼ cup butter
40 g/1½ oz/⅓ cup plain (all-purpose) flour
25 g/1 oz/¼ cup hazelnuts,
    roughly chopped
50 g/2 oz/½ cup flaked (sliced)
    almonds, chopped
50 g/2 oz/¼ cup glacé
    cherries, chopped
115 g/4 oz dark chocolate, melted,
    for coating

2 Remove the pan from the heat and add the flour, hazelnuts, almonds and cherries. Stir well.

3 Spoon small heaps of the mixture on to the baking sheets. Bake for about 10 minutes, until golden brown. Leave the cookies on the baking sheet until the edges begin to harden a little, then transfer to a wire rack to cool.

1 Preheat the oven to 180°C/350°F/ Gas 4. Line four baking sheets with baking parchment. Combine the sugar, honey, Grand Marnier and butter in a small pan and melt over a low heat.

VARIATION: You could use melted white chocolate for the zigzag decoration, if you like.

4 Spread the melted chocolate over one side of each florentine, using a kitchen knife. When it begins to set, drag a fork through to form wavy lines. Leave to set completely. Fill a piping (pastry) bag with the remaining melted chocolate, snip off the end and pipe zigzag lines over the plain side of the florentines.

Brandy Snaps

The combination of the crisp, light-as-air cookie and rich, brandy-flavoured creamy filling is magical.

Makes 16

INGREDIENTS
50 g/2 oz/¼ cup butter, at room temperature, plus extra for greasing
130 g/4½ oz/⅔ cup sugar
20 ml/4 tsp golden (light corn) syrup
40 g/1½ oz/⅓ cup plain (all-purpose) flour
2.5 ml/½ tsp ground ginger

FOR THE FILLING
250 ml/8 fl oz/ 1 cup whipping cream
30 ml/2 tbsp brandy

1 With an electric mixer, cream together the butter and sugar until light and fluffy, then beat in the syrup. Sift over the flour and ginger and mix to a rough dough.

2 Transfer the dough to a work surface and knead until smooth. Cover and chill in the refrigerator for 30 minutes.

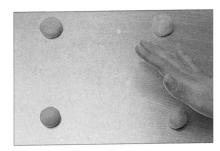

3 Preheat the oven to 190°C/375°F/Gas 5. Grease a baking sheet. Working in batches of four, form walnut-size balls of dough. Place far apart on the prepared sheet and flatten the balls slightly. Bake for about 10 minutes, or until golden and bubbling.

4 Remove from the oven and cool for a few moments. Working quickly, slide a metal spatula under each one, turn over and wrap around the handle of a wooden spoon (have four spoons ready). If they firm up too quickly, reheat for a few seconds to soften. When firm, slide the snaps off and place on a rack to cool.

5 When all the brandy snaps are cool, prepare the filling. Whip the cream and brandy until soft peaks form. Fill a piping (pastry) bag with the brandy cream. Pipe into each end of the brandy snaps just before serving.

Chocolate Marzipan Cookies

These crisp cookies – with a little almond surprise inside – are perfect for those with a sweet tooth.

Makes about 36

INGREDIENTS

200 g/7 oz/scant 1 cup unsalted (sweet) butter, softened, plus extra for greasing

200 g/7 oz/scant 1 cup light muscovado (brown) sugar

1 egg

300 g/11 oz/2⅔ cups plain (all-purpose) flour, plus extra for dusting

60 ml/4 tbsp unsweetened cocoa powder

200 g/7 oz white marzipan

115 g/4 oz white chocolate, broken into squares

3 Roll out about half the dough on a lightly floured surface to about 5 mm/¼ in thick. Using a 5 cm/2 in biscuit cutter, cut out rounds, re-rolling the dough as required until you have about 36 rounds.

1 Preheat the oven to 190°C/375°F/ Gas 5. Lightly grease two large baking sheets. Cream the butter with the sugar in a bowl until pale and fluffy. Add the egg and beat well.

2 Sift the flour and cocoa over the mixture. Stir in, first with a wooden spoon, then with clean hands, pressing the mixture together to make a fairly soft dough.

4 Cut the marzipan into about 36 equal pieces. Roll into balls, flatten slightly and place one on each round of dough. Roll out the remaining dough, cut out more rounds, then place on top of the almond paste. Press the dough edges to seal.

5 Bake for 10–12 minutes, or until the cookies have risen well and are beginning to crack on the surface. Leave on the baking sheet to cool slightly for about 2–3 minutes, then transfer to a wire rack to cool completely.

6 Melt the white chocolate, then either drizzle it over the biscuits to decorate or spoon into a paper piping bag and quickly pipe a design on them.

COOK'S TIP: If the dough is too sticky to roll, chill it for about 30 minutes, then try again.

Fudgy Glazed Chocolate Bars

For a simpler bar, omit the fudge glaze and dust with icing sugar instead.

Serves 8–10

INGREDIENTS
115 g/4 oz/½ cup unsalted (sweet) butter, cut
    into pieces, plus extra for greasing
250 g/9 oz dark (bittersweet) or plain
    (semisweet) chocolate, chopped
25 g/1 oz unsweetened chocolate, chopped
90 g/3½ oz/scant ½ cup light brown sugar
50 g/2 oz/¼ cup granulated sugar
2 eggs
15 ml/1 tbsp vanilla essence (extract)
65 g/2½ oz/9 tbsp plain (all-purpose) flour
115 g/4 oz/⅔ cup pecan nuts or walnuts,
    toasted and chopped
150 g/5 oz fine quality white chocolate,
    chopped into 5 mm/¼ in pieces
pecan halves, to decorate (optional)

FOR THE FUDGY CHOCOLATE GLAZE
175 g/6 oz plain (semisweet) or dark
    (bittersweet) chocolate, chopped
50 g/2 oz/¼ cup unsalted (sweet) butter
30 ml/2 tbsp corn or golden syrup
10 ml/2 tsp vanilla essence (extract)
5 ml/1 tsp instant coffee powder

1 Preheat the oven to 180°C/350°F/
Gas 4. Invert a 20 cm/8 in square cake
tin (pan) and mould a piece of foil
over it. Turn it over and line with the
moulded foil. Lightly grease the foil.

2 In a medium pan over a low heat,
melt the dark chocolates and butter
until smooth, stirring frequently.

3 Remove the pan from the heat.
Stir in the sugars and continue stirring
for 2 more minutes, until they dissolve.
Beat in the eggs and vanilla and stir in
the flour until just blended. Stir in the
pecan nuts or walnuts and white
chocolate. Pour the batter into the
prepared tin.

4 Bake for 20–25 minutes, or until
a cocktail stick (toothpick) inserted
5 cm/2 in from the centre comes out
with just a few crumbs attached (do
not overbake or it will be dry).
Remove the tin to a wire rack to cool
for about 30 minutes. Using the foil to
lift, remove the "cake" from the tin and
cool on the rack for at least 2 hours.

5 Prepare the glaze. In a medium pan over a medium heat, melt the chocolate, butter, syrup, vanilla essence and coffee powder, stirring frequently, until smooth. Remove from the heat. Chill for 1 hour, or until thickened and spreadable.

6 Invert the "cake" on to the wire rack and remove the foil. Turn top-side up. Using a metal spatula, spread a thick layer of fudgy glaze over the top. Chill for 1 hour, until set. Cut into bars. If you wish, top each with a pecan half.

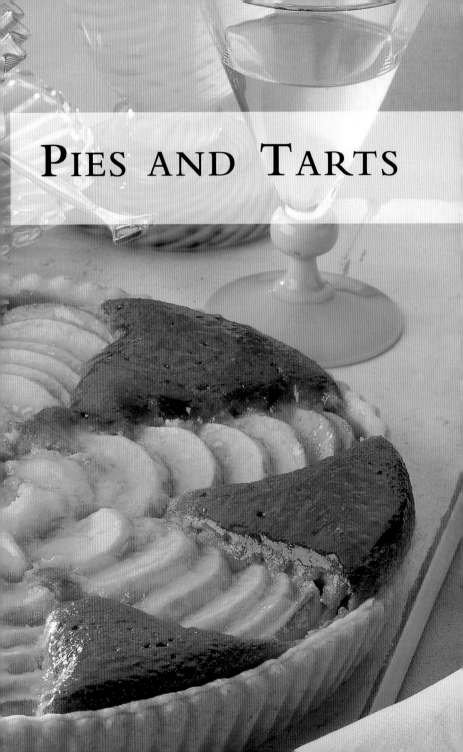

PIES AND TARTS

French Apple Tart

This classic tart is delicious served warm or cold, either on its own or with whipped cream for a special treat.

Serves 8

INGREDIENTS
350 g/12 oz sweet shortcrust pastry,
    defrosted if frozen

FOR THE FILLING
115 g/4 oz/½ cup butter, softened
115 g/4 oz/½ cup caster (superfine) sugar
2 large (US extra large) eggs, beaten
115 g/4 oz/1 cup ground almonds
25 g/1 oz/¼ cup plain (all-purpose)
    flour

FOR THE TOPPING
3 eating apples
60 ml/4 tbsp apricot jam
15 ml/1 tbsp water

1 Preheat the oven to 190°C/375°F/ Gas 5. Place a baking sheet in the oven to heat. Roll out the pastry on a lightly floured surface and line a 23 cm/9 in fluted flan tin (tart pan).

2 To make the filling, beat all the ingredients together until light and fluffy. Spoon into the pastry case (pie shell) and level the surface.

VARIATION: A redcurrant glaze would also look good on this tart. Warm redcurrant jelly with a little lemon juice. Brush over the apples.

3 To make the topping, peel and core the apples and cut in half. Place each half, cut side down, on a board. Using a sharp, fine knife, slice the apples thinly, keeping the shape, then press down lightly to fan each apple half in a row.

4 Using a palette knife or metal spatula, carefully transfer each row of apple slices to the tart, arranging them on top of the filling so that they resemble the spokes of a wheel. You may need to overlap the slices in the middle slightly to fit. Press the slices down well into the filling to secure.

5 Warm the apricot jam with the water, then press the mixture through a sieve (strainer) into a small bowl. Brush half the jam glaze over the apples. Place the tin on the baking sheet and bake the tart for 35 minutes or until the pastry is golden and the apples have started to singe slightly.

6 Rewarm the remaining jam glaze and brush it over the apples. Let the tart cool slightly before serving.

Pear Tarte Tatin with Cardamom

Crispy puff pastry snugly encloses tasty caramelized pears in this spicy upside-down tart.

Serves 4

INGREDIENTS
50 g/2 oz/¼ cup unsalted (sweet)
   butter, softened
50 g/2 oz/¼ cup caster (superfine) sugar
seeds from 10 cardamoms
225 g/8 oz puff pastry, thawed if frozen
3 ripe pears, peeled, cored and
   halved lengthways

1 Preheat the oven to 220°C/425°F/ Gas 7. Spread the butter over the base of an 18 cm/7 in heavy-based cake tin (pan) or an ovenproof omelette pan. Spread the sugar evenly over the base of the tin or pan. Scatter the cardamom seeds over the sugar.

2 On a floured surface, roll out the puff pastry to a round slightly larger than the tin or pan. Prick the pastry lightly, then transfer it to a baking sheet and chill while you prepare the filling.

3 Arrange the pears, rounded side down, on the butter and sugar. Set the cake tin or omelette pan over a medium heat until the sugar melts and begins to bubble. If any areas are browning more than others, move the pan, but do not stir.

4 As soon as the sugar has caramelized, remove the tin or pan carefully from the heat. Place the pastry on top, tucking the edges down the side of the pan. Transfer to the oven and bake for 25 minutes, until well risen and golden.

5 Leave the tart in the tin or pan for 2–3 minutes until the juices have stopped bubbling. Invert the tin over a plate and shake to release the tart. It may be necessary to slide a spatula underneath the pears to loosen them. Serve the tart warm.

Lemon Tart

This is one of the classic French tarts, and it is difficult to beat: a rich lemon curd, encased in crisp pastry.

Serves 6

INGREDIENTS
225 g/8 oz/2 cups plain (all-purpose) flour
115 g/4 oz/½ cup butter, diced
30 ml/2 tbsp icing (confectioners') sugar
1 egg, beaten
5 ml/1 tsp vanilla essence (extract)
6 eggs, beaten
350 g/12 oz/1¾ cups caster (superfine) sugar
115 g/4 oz/½ cup unsalted (sweet) butter
grated rind and juice of 4 lemons
icing (confectioners') sugar, for dusting

1 Preheat the oven to 200°C/400°F/ Gas 6. Sift the flour into a bowl, add the diced butter, and work with your fingertips until the mixture resembles fine breadcrumbs. Stir in the icing sugar.

2 Add the egg, vanilla essence and a scant tablespoon of cold water, then work to a dough.

3 Roll out the pastry on a floured surface and use to line a 23 cm/9 in tart tin (pan). Line with foil or baking parchment and fill with baking beans. Bake for 10 minutes.

4 For the filling, put the eggs, sugar and butter into a pan and stir over a low heat until the sugar has dissolved. Add the lemon rind and juice, and continue cooking, stirring, until the lemon curd has thickened slightly.

5 Pour the mixture into the pastry case. Bake for 20 minutes, until just set. Transfer to a wire rack to cool. Dust with icing sugar before serving.

Pecan Pie

Melt-in-the-mouth pastry encloses the sweet, rich filling of this popular American pie. It's delicious served with cream or ice cream.

Serves 6

INGREDIENTS

200 g/7 oz/1¾ cups plain (all-purpose) flour
115 g/4 oz/½ cup butter
30–60 ml/2–4 tbsp iced water
3 eggs
5 ml/1 tsp vanilla essence (extract)
200 g/7 oz/¾ cup soft dark brown sugar
60 ml/4 tbsp golden (light corn) syrup
50 g/2 oz/4 tbsp butter, melted
115 g/4 oz/1 cup chopped pecan kernels, plus 12 pecan halves
salt
whipped cream or vanilla ice cream, to serve

1 Mix the flour with a pinch of salt, then rub in the butter with the fingertips until the mixture resembles fine breadcrumbs. Add iced water a little at a time, mixing first with a fork. Gather into a dough.

2 Wrap the dough in clear film (plastic wrap) and chill in the refrigerator for 30 minutes. Preheat the oven to 190°C/375°F/Gas 5. Grease a 20 cm/8 in loose-based flan tin (tart pan). Roll out the pastry and use to line the tin.

3 Run the rolling pin over the top of the tin to cut off the surplus pastry.

4 Prick the pastry base and line with foil and baking beans. Bake blind for 15 minutes, then remove the foil and bake for a further 5 minutes. Take the pastry case from the oven and lower the temperature to 180°C/350°F/Gas 4.

5 Meanwhile, to make the filling, beat the eggs lightly with a pinch of salt and vanilla essence, then beat in the sugar, syrup and melted butter. Mix in the chopped pecans.

6 Spread the mixture in the pastry case and bake for 15 minutes. Remove from the oven and stud with the pecan halves in a circle.

7 Return to the oven and bake for a further 20–25 minutes until cooked through. Cool the pie for 10–15 minutes and serve warm with whipped cream or a scoop of vanilla ice cream.

Chocolate Pine Nut Tart

Lemon rind could be used instead of orange and a combination of white and plain chocolate substituted for all plain.

Serves 8

INGREDIENTS
200 g/7½ oz/scant 2 cups plain
   (all-purpose) flour
50 g/2 oz/¼ cup caster (superfine) sugar
pinch of salt
grated rind of ½ orange
115 g/4 oz/½ cup unsalted (sweet) butter
3 egg yolks, lightly beaten
15–30 ml/1–2 tbsp iced water

FOR THE FILLING
2 eggs
40 g/1½ oz/3 tbsp caster (superfine) sugar
grated rind of 1 orange
15 ml/1 tbsp orange-flavour liqueur
250 ml/8 fl oz/1 cup whipping cream
115 g/4 oz plain (semisweet) chocolate,
   chopped
75 g/3 oz/¾ cup pine nuts, toasted

FOR THE DECORATION
1 orange
50 g/2 oz/¼ cup granulated sugar
120 ml/4 fl oz/½ cup water

1 In a food processor, blend the flour, sugar, salt and orange rind. Add the butter and process for 20–30 seconds until it resembles coarse crumbs. Add the yolks and pulse until it begins to combine; do not allow to form a ball. If it is dry, add 15–30 ml/1–2 tbsp iced water, little by little, just until it holds.

2 Turn on to a lightly floured surface. Knead gently until blended. Shape into a disc and wrap in clear film (plastic wrap). Chill for 2–3 hours.

3 Lightly butter a 23 cm/9 in, loose-based tart tin (pan). Soften the dough for 5–10 minutes. On a well-floured surface, roll out the dough to a 28 cm/11 in round, about 3 mm/⅛ in thick and line the tin.

4 Roll a rolling pin over the edge to cut off excess dough. Now press the thicker top edge against the side of the tin to form a rim slightly higher than the tin. Prick the base with a fork. Chill for 1 hour. Preheat the oven to 200°C/400°F/Gas 6.

5 Line the pastry with baking parchment and baking beans and bake for 5 minutes. Lift out the paper and beans and bake for 5 more minutes. Cool slightly on a rack. Lower the heat to 180°C/350°F/Gas 4.

6 To make the filling, beat the eggs, sugar, rind and liqueur together. Blend in the cream. Sprinkle the chocolate and pine nuts evenly over the bottom of the pastry. Place the tin on a baking sheet and gently pour the egg mixture into the case. Bake for 20–30 minutes until the pastry is golden and the custard set. Cool slightly then transfer the tart to a wire rack.

7 To make the decoration, remove thin strips of orange rind and cut into julienne strips. Boil for 5–8 minutes with the sugar and water, until the syrup is thickened, then stir in 15 ml/ 1 tbsp cold water to halt the cooking.

8 Carefully brush the tart with the orange-sugar syrup and arrange julienne orange strips over the top.

Italian Chocolate Ricotta Pie

This delectable pie has chocolate in both pastry and filling, and the sherry makes it even more special.

Serves 6

INGREDIENTS
225 g/8 oz/2 cups plain (all-purpose) flour
30 ml/2 tbsp unsweetened cocoa powder,
    plus extra for sprinkling
60 ml/4 tbsp caster (superfine) sugar
115 g/4 oz/½ cup unsalted (sweet) butter
60 ml/4 tbsp dry sherry

FOR THE FILLING
2 egg yolks
115 g/4 oz/generous ½ cup caster
    (superfine) sugar
500 g/1¼ lb/2½ cups ricotta cheese
finely grated rind of 1 lemon
90 ml/6 tbsp dark (bittersweet)
    chocolate chips
75 ml/5 tbsp chopped mixed (candied) peel
45 ml/3 tbsp chopped angelica

1 Preheat the oven to 200°C/400°F/ Gas 6. Sift the flour and cocoa into a bowl, then stir in the sugar. Rub in the butter until the mixture resembles breadcrumbs, then work in the sherry, using your fingertips, until the mixture binds to a firm dough.

2 Roll out three-quarters of the pastry on a lightly floured surface and use it to line a 24 cm/9½ in loose-based flan tin (tart pan).

3 To make the filling, beat the egg yolks and sugar in a bowl, then beat in the ricotta cheese to mix thoroughly. Stir in the lemon rind, chocolate chips, mixed peel and angelica.

4 Scrape the ricotta mixture into the pastry case and level the surface. Roll out the remaining pastry and cut into strips, then arrange these in a lattice over the pie.

VARIATION: Instead of sherry you could use brandy or Amaretto.

5 Bake for 15 minutes, then lower the heat to 180°C/350°F/Gas 4 and cook for a further 30–35 minutes until the pastry is golden brown and the filling is firm. Cool in the tin. Sprinkle with cocoa powder just before serving at room temperature.

COOK'S TIP: This pie is best served at room temperature, so if you make it in advance, chill it when cool, then bring to room temperature for about 30 minutes before serving.

Chocolate Truffle Tart

Try serving this rich tart with cream, for the ultimate indulgence.

Serves 12

INGREDIENTS
150 g/5 oz/1¼ cups plain (all-purpose) flour
25 g/1 oz/¼ cup unsweetened cocoa powder
50 g/2 oz/¼ cup caster (superfine) sugar
2.5 ml/½ tsp salt
115 g/4 oz/½ cup chilled unsalted (sweet)
   butter, cut in pieces
1 egg yolk
15–30 ml/1–2 tbsp iced water
25 g/1 oz white or milk chocolate, melted

FOR THE TRUFFLE FILLING
335 ml/11 fl oz/1⅓ cups double
   (heavy) cream
350 g/12 oz couverture or fine-quality plain
   (semisweet) chocolate, chopped
50 g/2 oz/4 tbsp unsalted (sweet) butter, cut
   in pieces
30 ml/2 tbsp brandy or liqueur

1 Sift the flour and cocoa into a bowl. In a food processor fitted with metal blade, process the flour mixture, sugar and salt to blend. Add the butter and process for 15–20 seconds until the mixture resembles coarse breadcrumbs.

2 In a bowl, lightly beat the yolk with the water. Add to the flour mixture and, using the pulse action, process to a dough. Turn out on to clear film (plastic wrap), shape the dough into a flat disc and wrap tightly. Chill for 1–2 hours until firm.

3 Lightly grease a 23 cm/9 in, loose-based tart tin (pan). Soften the dough for 5–10 minutes, then roll out between sheets of waxed paper to a 28 cm/11 in round, about 5 mm/¼ in thick. Peel off the top sheet and invert into the tin. Remove the bottom sheet. Ease the dough on to the base and sides of the tin. Prick the base and chill for 1 hour.

4 Preheat the oven to 180°C/350°F/ Gas 4. Line the pastry with baking parchment and fill with beans. Bake for 5–7 minutes, then lift out the paper and beans and bake for 5–7 minutes until just set. (The pastry may look underdone on the bottom, but it will dry out.) Cool on a wire rack.

5 For the truffle filling bring the double cream to the boil in a pan over medium heat. Remove from the heat and stir in the couverture or plain chocolate until melted. Stir in the butter and liqueur. Strain evenly into the pastry, but avoid touching.

6 Spoon the melted chocolate into a paper cone and cut a tip about 5 mm/ ¼ in in diameter. Drop rounds of chocolate over the surface of the tart and draw the point of a skewer or cocktail stick (toothpick) through the chocolate to produce a marbled effect. Chill for 2–3 hours until set. Allow the tart to soften at room temperature for about 30 minutes before serving.

Mississippi Mud Pie

This open-topped pie has three layers of "mud": dark chocolate, golden, rum-flavoured custard and whipped cream – sheer ecstasy!

Serves 6–8

INGREDIENTS
250 g/9 oz/2¼ cups plain (all-purpose) flour
150 g/5 oz/10 tbsp unsalted (sweet) butter
2 egg yolks
15–30 ml/1–2 tbsp iced water

FOR THE FILLING
3 eggs, separated
20 ml/4 tsp cornflour (cornstarch)
75 g/3 oz/scant ½ cup golden caster (superfine) sugar
400 ml/14 fl oz/1⅔ cups milk
150 g/5 oz plain (semisweet) chocolate, broken into squares
5 ml/1 tsp pure vanilla essence (extract)
1 sachet powdered gelatine
45 ml/3 tbsp water
30 ml/2 tsp dark rum

FOR THE TOPPING
175 ml/6 fl oz/¾ cup double (heavy) or whipping cream
chocolate curls

1 Sift the flour into a large bowl and rub in the butter until the mixture resembles coarse breadcrumbs. Stir in the egg yolks with just enough iced water to bind the mixture to a soft pliable dough. Roll out on a lightly floured surface and line a deep, 23 cm/9 in flan tin (tart pan). Chill for about 30 minutes.

2 Preheat the oven to 190°C/375°F/ Gas 5. Prick the pastry case all over with a fork, cover with baking parchment weighed down with baking beans and bake blind for 10 minutes. Remove the baking beans and paper, return to the oven and bake for a further 10 minutes until the pastry is crisp and golden. Cool in the tin.

3 To make the filling, mix the egg yolks, cornflour and 30 ml/2 tbsp of the sugar in a bowl. Heat the milk in a pan until almost boiling, then beat into the egg mixture. Return to the clean pan and stir over a low heat until the custard has thickened and is smooth. Pour half the custard into a heatproof bowl.

4 Melt the chocolate in a heatproof bowl over hot water, then stir into the custard in the bowl, with the vanilla essence. Spread in the pastry case, cover closely to prevent the formation of a skin, cool, then chill until set.

5 Sprinkle the gelatine over the water in a small bowl, leave until spongy, then place over simmering water until all the gelatine has dissolved. Stir into the remaining custard, with the rum. Whisk the egg whites in a clean, grease-free bowl until stiff peaks form, whisk in the remaining sugar, then fold quickly into the custard before it sets.

6 Spoon the mixture over the chocolate custard to cover completely. Chill until set, then remove the pie from the tin and place on a large serving plate.

7 Spread whipped cream over the top, sprinkle with the chocolate curls and serve.

Chocolate Profiteroles

These choux pastry puffs are extremely easy to make, but look very impressive. This unusual version includes a rich chocolate glaze.

Makes 12 large or 24 small profiteroles

INGREDIENTS

150 g/5 oz/¾ cup plain (all-purpose) flour
25 g/1 oz/¼ cup unsweetened cocoa powder
250 ml/8 fl oz/1 cup water
2.5 ml/½ tsp salt
15 ml/1 tbsp sugar
115 g/4 oz/½ cup unsalted sweet butter
4 or 5 eggs
300 ml/½ pint/1¼ cups whipping cream
15 ml/1 tbsp each unsweetened cocoa and
  hot water, blended together and cooled

FOR THE SAUCE

300 ml/½ pint/1¼ cups whipping cream
50 g/2 oz/4 tbsp unsalted (sweet) butter
225 g/8 oz plain (semisweet) chocolate
15 ml/1 tbsp golden (light corn) syrup
5 ml/1 tsp vanilla essence (extract)

1 Preheat the oven to 220°C/425°F/ Gas 7. Lightly grease one or two large baking sheets. Sift together the flour and cocoa into a bowl. Bring the water, salt, sugar and butter to the boil in a pan.

2 Remove from the heat and add the flour mixture all at once, stirring vigorously until the mixture pulls away from the side of the pan. Return the pan to the heat for 1 minute, beating constantly. Remove from the heat.

3 Beat in four of the eggs, one at a time. If the mixture is too dry, beat the fifth egg lightly and add to the dough a little at a time until you reach a dropping consistency. Spoon the mixture into a large icing bag fitted with a large star nozzle. Pipe 12 or 24 mounds 5 cm/2 in apart on the baking sheet.

4 Bake for 35–40 minutes, until puffed and firm. Using a serrated knife, slice off the top third of each cake. Place cut side up on the baking sheet and return to the switched-off oven for 5–10 minutes to dry out. Remove to a wire rack to cool.

5 Whip the cream and add the cocoa mixture. Using a piping (icing) bag, fill each puff base with cream, then cover each with its top. Arrange on a serving plate.

6 For the sauce, break the chocolate into squares and put it in a pan over a low heat with the cream, butter, syrup and vanilla. Stir until smooth. Remove from the heat and cool for 20–30 minutes, until slightly thickened. Pour a little sauce over each of the profiteroles and serve warm or cold.

Red Grape & Cheese Tartlets

Fruit and cheese form a natural combination in this simple recipe. Look out for red grapes, which tend to be sweeter than black grapes.

Makes 6

INGREDIENTS
350 g/12 oz sweet shortcrust pastry, defrosted if frozen
225 g/8 oz/1 cup curd (farmers') cheese
150 ml/¼ pint/⅔ cup double (heavy) cream
2.5 ml/½ tsp vanilla essence (extract)
30 ml/2 tbsp icing (confectioners') sugar
200 g/7 oz/2 cups red grapes, halved, seeded if necessary
60 ml/4 tbsp apricot conserve
15 ml/1 tbsp water

1 Preheat the oven to 200°C/400°F/ Gas 6. On a lightly floured surface, roll out the pastry and use to line six deep, 9 cm/3½ in, fluted individual tartlet tins (muffin pans), pressing well into the sides. Trim off any excess pastry with a knife or scissors. Prick the bases with a fork and line with baking parchment and baking beans.

2 Bake for 10 minutes, remove the paper and beans, then return the cases to the oven for 5 minutes until golden and fully cooked. Remove from the tins and cool on a wire rack.

3 Beat the curd cheese, double cream, vanilla essence and icing sugar in a bowl. Divide the mixture among the pastry cases. Smooth the surface and arrange the halved grapes on top.

4 Sieve (strain) the apricot conserve into a pan. Add the water and heat, stirring, until smooth. Spoon over the grapes. Cool, then chill before serving.

VARIATIONS: Use cranberry jelly or redcurrant jelly for the glaze. There is no need to sieve. Also vary the fruit topping: try blackberries, blueberries, raspberries, strawberries, kiwi fruit, banana or pineapple slices.

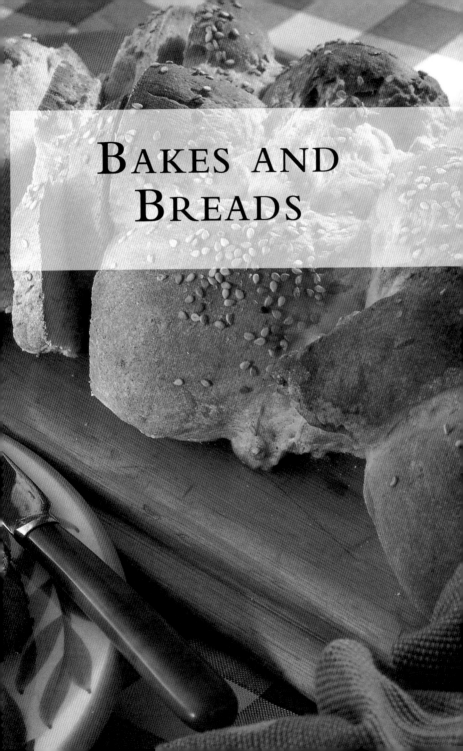

BAKES AND BREADS

Fresh Blueberry Muffins

Make these popular American treats in paper cases for moister muffins.

Makes 12

INGREDIENTS
275 g/10 oz/2½ cups plain (all-purpose) flour
15 ml/1 tbsp baking powder
75 g/3 oz/scant ½ cup caster
   (superfine) sugar
250 ml/8 fl oz/1 cup milk
3 eggs, beaten
115 g/4 oz/½ cup butter, melted
few drops of vanilla essence (extract)
225 g/8 oz/2 cups fresh or
   frozen blueberries

FOR THE TOPPING
50 g/2 oz/½ cup pecan nuts,
   coarsely chopped
30 ml/2 tbsp demerara (raw) sugar

1 Preheat the oven to 200°C/400°F/ Gas 6. Stand 12 paper muffin cases in a muffin tin (pan) or simply grease the tin thoroughly.

2 Sift the flour and baking powder into a large bowl. Stir in the caster sugar. Mix the milk, eggs, melted butter and vanilla essence in a jug (pitcher) and whisk lightly. Add to the flour mixture and fold together lightly.

3 Fold in the blueberries, then divide the mixture among the muffin cases. Scatter a few nuts and a little demerara sugar over the top of each. Bake for 20–25 minutes or until the muffins are well risen and golden. Remove from the tin and cool slightly on a wire rack.

Drop Scones

Serve these scones while still warm, with butter and jam.

Makes 24

INGREDIENTS
225 g/8 oz/2 cups self-raising
   (self-rising) flour
50 g/2 oz/4 tbsp caster
   (superfine) sugar
50 g/2 oz/4 tbsp butter, melted
1 egg
300 ml/½ pint/1¼ cups milk
15 g/½ oz/1 tbsp hard white fat

1 Mix the flour and sugar together in a bowl. Add the melted butter and egg with two-thirds of the milk. Mix to a smooth batter – it should be thin enough to have a level surface.

2 Heat a griddle or a heavy-based frying pan and wipe it with a little hard white fat. When it is hot, drop in spoonfuls of the mixture. When bubbles come to the surface of the scones, flip them over to cook until golden on the other side.

3 Remove the scones from the pan and keep them warm, wrapped in a dishtowel, while you cook the rest of the mixture. Serve warm.

VARIATION: Add a little ground cinnamon with the flour if you like lightly spiced pancakes.

Cheese & Chive Scones

Feta cheese, used here instead of butter, gives these tangy savoury scones a lovely light texture and delicious flavour.

Makes 9

INGREDIENTS

115 g/4 oz/1 cup self-raising (self-rising) flour
150 g/5 oz/1 cup self-raising (self-rising) wholemeal (whole-wheat) flour
2.5 ml/½ tsp salt
75 g/3 oz feta cheese
15 ml/1 tbsp fresh chives
150 ml/¼ pint/⅔ cup milk, plus extra for glazing
1.5 ml/¼ tsp cayenne pepper

1 Preheat the oven to 200°C/400°F/ Gas 6. Sift the two different flours and the salt into a large mixing bowl, adding any bran that has been left over from the flour in the sieve.

2 Crumble the feta cheese and rub into the dry ingredients. Stir in the chives, then add the milk and mix to a soft dough.

3 Turn the dough out on to a floured surface and lightly knead until smooth. Roll out to a 2 cm/¾ in thickness and stamp out nine scones with a 6 cm/ 2½ in cookie cutter.

4 Transfer the scones to a non–stick baking sheet. Brush with a little milk, then sprinkle with a light dusting of cayenne pepper.

5 Bake the scones in the oven for 15 minutes, or until golden brown. Serve warm or cold.

Brioche

Rich and buttery, yet light and airy, this wonderful loaf captures the
essence of the classic French bread.

Makes 1 loaf

INGREDIENTS
350 g/12 oz/3 cups unbleached strong white
   bread flour
2.5 ml/½ tsp salt
15 g/½ oz fresh yeast
60 ml/4 tbsp lukewarm milk
3 eggs
175 g/6 oz/¾ cup butter, softened
25 g/1 oz/2 tbsp caster (superfine) sugar

FOR THE GLAZE
1 egg yolk
15 ml/1 tbsp milk

1 Sift the flour and salt into a large
bowl and make a well in the centre.
Stir together the yeast and milk. Add
the yeast mixture to the well in the
flour mixture with the eggs and mix
together to form a soft dough.

2 Using your hand, beat the dough
for 4–5 minutes until smooth and
elastic. Cream the butter and sugar
together. Gradually add the butter
mixture to the dough in small
amounts, making sure each amount is
incorporated before adding more. Beat
until smooth, shiny and elastic, then
cover the bowl and leave in a warm
place to rise for 1–2 hours.

3 Lightly knock back (punch down)
the dough, then cover and place in the
refrigerator for 8 hours or overnight.

4 Lightly grease a 1.6 litre/2¾ pint/
scant 7 cup brioche mould. Turn the
dough out on to a lightly floured
surface. Cut off almost a quarter, shape
the rest into a ball and place in the
mould. Shape the reserved dough into
an elongated egg shape. Using two or
three fingers, make a hole in the centre
of the large ball of dough. Gently press
the narrow end of the egg-shaped
dough into the hole.

5 Mix together the egg yolk and milk for the glaze and brush a little over the brioche. Cover and leave in a warm place to rise for 1½–2 hours.

6 Meanwhile, preheat the oven to 230°C/450°F/Gas 8. Brush the brioche with the remaining glaze and bake for 10 minutes. Reduce the oven temperature to 190°C/375°F/Gas 5 and bake for a further 20–25 minutes, or until golden. Turn out on to a wire rack to cool.

Orange & Coriander Brioches

The warm, spicy flavour of coriander combines especially well with orange in these tempting little rolls.

Makes 12

INGREDIENTS
225 g/8 oz/2 cups strong white bread flour
10 ml/2 tsp easy-blend (rapid-rise)
    dried yeast
2.5 ml/½ tsp salt
15 ml/1 tbsp caster (superfine) sugar
10 ml/2 tsp coriander seeds,
    coarsely ground
grated rind of 1 orange
2 eggs, beaten
50 g/2 oz/4 tbsp unsalted (sweet)
    butter, melted
1 small (US medium) egg, beaten, to glaze
fine strips of orange rind,
    to decorate (optional)

1 Grease 12 individual brioche tins (pans). Sift the flour into a mixing bowl and stir in the yeast, salt, sugar, ground coriander seeds and orange rind.

2 Make a well in the centre of the mixture, pour in 30 ml/2 tbsp hand-hot water, the eggs and melted butter. Beat to form a soft dough.

3 Turn out the dough on to a lightly floured surface and knead it for 5 minutes until smooth and elastic. Return to the clean, lightly oiled bowl, cover with a damp dishtowel and leave in a warm place for 1 hour until doubled in bulk.

4 Turn on to a floured surface, knead again briefly and roll into a sausage. Cut into 12 pieces. Break off a quarter of each piece and set aside. Shape the larger pieces of dough into balls and place in the prepared tins.

5 With a floured wooden spoon, press a hole in each dough ball. Shape each small piece of dough into a little plug and press into the holes.

6 Place the tins on a baking sheet. Cover with a damp dishtowel and leave in a warm place until the dough rises almost to the top of the tins. Brush the brioches with beaten egg.

7 Preheat the oven to 220°C/425°F/ Gas 7. Bake the risen brioches for 15 minutes until golden brown. Scatter over a few fine strips of orange rind to decorate, if you like, and serve the brioches warm.

COOK'S TIP: These individual brioches look particularly attractive if they are made in special brioche tins (pans). However, they can also be made in bun tins or muffin tins.

Panettone

This classic bread can be found throughout Italy around Christmas. It is surprisingly light, even though it is rich with butter and dried fruit.

Makes 1 loaf

INGREDIENTS
400 g/14 oz/3½ cups unbleached strong
    white bread flour
2.5 ml/½ tsp salt
15 g/½ oz fresh yeast
120 ml/4 fl oz/½ cup lukewarm milk
2 eggs
2 egg yolks
75 g/3 oz/6 tbsp caster (superfine) sugar
150 g/5 oz/⅔ cup butter, softened
115 g/4 oz/⅔ cup mixed chopped
    (candied) peel
75 g/3 oz/½ cup raisins
melted butter, for brushing

1 Using a double layer of greaseproof paper, line and butter a 20 cm/8 in wide/15 cm/6 in deep cake tin or soufflé dish. Finish the paper 7.5 cm/ 3 in above the top of the tin.

2 Sift the flour and salt into a large bowl. Make a well in the centre. Cream the yeast with 60 ml/4 tbsp of the milk, then mix in the remainder.

3 Pour the yeast mixture into the centre of the flour, add the whole eggs and mix in sufficient flour to make a thick batter. Sprinkle a little of the remaining flour over the top and leave the batter to sponge, in a warm place, for 30 minutes.

4 Add the egg yolks and sugar and mix to a soft dough. Work in the softened butter, then turn out on to a lightly floured surface and knead for 5 minutes, until smooth and elastic. Place in a lightly oiled bowl, cover and leave to rise for 1½–2 hours.

5 Knock back (punch down) the dough and turn out on to a lightly floured surface. Gently knead in the peel and raisins. Shape into a ball and place in the prepared tin. Cover and leave to rise for about 1 hour.

6 Meanwhile, preheat the oven to 190°C/375°F/Gas 5. Brush the surface with melted butter, and cut a cross in the top using a sharp knife. Bake for 20 minutes, then reduce the oven temperature to 180°C/350°F/Gas 4. Brush the top with butter again and bake for a further 25–30 minutes, or until golden.

7 Allow the panettone to cool in the tin for 5–10 minutes, then turn it out on to a wire rack to cool.

COOK'S TIP: Once the dough has been enriched with butter, do not put to rise in too warm a place or the loaf will become greasy.

Greek Easter Bread

Traditionally decorated with red-dyed eggs, this bread is made by bakers and in homes throughout Greece at Easter.

Makes 1 loaf

INGREDIENTS
25 g/1 oz fresh yeast
15–30 ml/1–2 tbsp lukewarm water
120 ml/4 fl oz/½ cup lukewarm milk
675 g/1½ lb/6 cups strong white bread flour
2 eggs, beaten
2.5 ml/½ tsp caraway seeds
15 ml/1 tbsp caster (superfine) sugar
15 ml/1 tbsp brandy
50 g/2 oz/4 tbsp butter, melted
1 egg white, beaten
50 g/2 oz/½ cup split almonds

FOR THE EGGS
3 eggs
1.5 ml/¼ tsp bright red food
   colouring paste
15 ml/1 tbsp white wine vinegar
5 ml/1 tsp water
5 ml/1 tsp olive oil

1 First make the egg decoration. Place the eggs in a pan of water and bring to the boil. Allow to boil gently for 10 minutes.

2 Meanwhile, mix the red food colouring, vinegar, water and olive oil in a shallow bowl. Remove the eggs from the pan, place on a wire rack for a few seconds to dry, then roll in the colouring mixture. Return to the rack to cool and dry.

3 Crumble the yeast into a bowl. Mix with the water until softened. Add the milk and 115 g/4 oz/1 cup of the flour and mix to a creamy consistency. Cover and leave in a warm place for 1 hour.

4 Sift the remaining flour into a large bowl and make a well in the centre. Pour the yeast mixture into the well and draw in a little of the flour from the sides. Add the eggs, caraway seeds, sugar and brandy. Incorporate the remaining flour, until the mixture begins to form a dough.

5 Mix in the melted butter. Turn the dough on to a floured surface and knead for about 10 minutes, until smooth. Return to the bowl, cover and leave to rise for 3 hours.

6 Preheat the oven to 180°C/350°F/ Gas 4. Knock back (punch down) the dough, turn on to a floured surface and knead for 2 minutes.

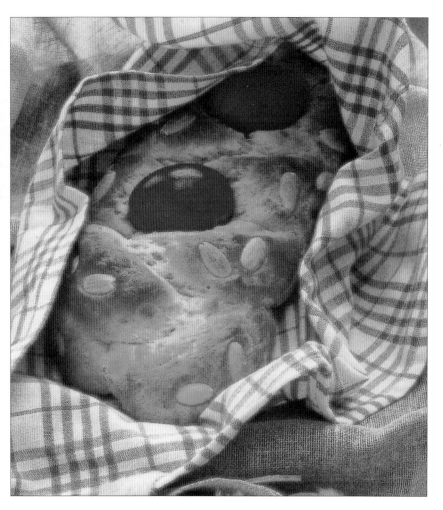

7 Divide the dough into three pieces and roll each piece into a long sausage shape. Make a braid and place the loaf on a greased baking sheet.

8 Tuck the ends under, brush with the egg white and decorate with the eggs and split almonds. Bake for about 1 hour. Cool on a wire rack.

Twelfth Night Bread

The traditional version of this Spanish bread contains a dried bean hidden inside – the lucky recipient is declared the king of the festival!

Makes 1 loaf

INGREDIENTS
450 g/1 lb/4 cups unbleached strong white
    bread flour
2.5 ml/½ tsp salt
25 g/1 oz fresh yeast
140 ml/scant ¼ pint/scant ⅔ cup mixed
    lukewarm milk and water
75 g/3 oz/6 tbsp butter
75 g/3 oz/6 tbsp caster (superfine) sugar
10 ml/2 tsp finely grated lemon rind
10 ml/2 tsp finely grated orange rind
2 eggs
15 ml/1 tbsp brandy
15 ml/1 tbsp orange flower water
dried bean (optional)
1 egg white, lightly beaten, for glazing

FOR THE DECORATION
a mixture of candied and glacé fruit slices
flaked (sliced) almonds

1 Lightly grease a large baking sheet. Sift the flour and salt into a large bowl. Make a well in the centre.

2 In a bowl, mix the yeast with the milk and water until the yeast has dissolved. Pour into the well and stir in enough of the flour to make a thick batter. Sprinkle a little of the remaining flour over the top of the batter and leave to sponge, in a warm place, for about 15 minutes, or until frothy.

3 Beat the butter and sugar together in a bowl until soft and creamy, then set aside.

4 Add the citrus rinds, eggs, brandy and orange flower water to the flour mixture and use a wooden spoon to mix to a sticky dough.

5 Using one hand, beat the mixture until it forms a fairly smooth dough. Gradually beat in the reserved butter mixture and beat for a few minutes until the dough is smooth and elastic. Cover and leave to rise for about 1½ hours.

6 Knock back (punch down) the dough and turn out on to a lightly floured surface. Gently knead for 2–3 minutes, incorporating the lucky bean, if using. Using a rolling pin, roll out the dough into a long strip measuring about 65 x 13 cm/26 x 5 in.

7 Roll up the dough from one long side like a Swiss jelly roll to make a long sausage shape. Place seam side down on the prepared baking sheet and seal the ends together. Cover and leave to rise for 1–1½ hours.

8 Meanwhile, preheat the oven to 180°C/350°F/Gas 4. Brush the dough ring with lightly beaten egg white and decorate with candied and glacé fruit slices, pushing them slightly into the dough. Sprinkle with almond flakes and bake for 30–35 minutes, or until risen and golden. Cool on a wire rack.

Malt Loaf

This is a rich and sticky loaf. If it lasts long enough to go stale, try toasting it for a delicious tea-time treat.

Makes 1 loaf

INGREDIENTS
150 ml/¼ pint/⅔ cup lukewarm milk
5 ml/1 tsp dried yeast
pinch of caster (superfine) sugar
350 g/12 oz/3 cups plain (all-purpose) flour
1.5 ml/¼ tsp salt
30 ml/2 tbsp light muscovado
  (brown) sugar
175 g/6 oz/generous 1 cup sultanas
  (golden raisins)
15 ml/1 tbsp sunflower oil
45 ml/3 tbsp malt extract

FOR THE GLAZE
30 ml/2 tbsp caster (superfine) sugar
30 ml/2 tbsp water

1 Pour the milk into a bowl. Sprinkle the yeast on top and add the sugar. Leave for 30 minutes, until frothy. Sift the flour and salt into a mixing bowl, stir in the muscovado sugar and sultanas, and make a well in the centre.

2 Add the yeast mixture together with the oil and the malt extract. Gradually incorporate the flour from the sides and mix to a soft dough, adding a little extra milk if necessary to achieve the right consistency.

3 Turn on to a floured surface and knead for about 5 minutes, until smooth and elastic. Grease a 450 g/ 1 lb loaf tin (pan).

4 Shape the dough and place it in the prepared tin. Cover and leave in a warm place to rise for 1–2 hours. Preheat the oven to 190°C/375°F/ Gas 5.

5 Bake the loaf for 30–35 minutes, until golden and ready. Meanwhile, prepare the glaze by dissolving the sugar in the water in a small pan. Bring to the boil, stirring, then lower the heat and simmer for 1 minute. Place the loaf on a wire rack and brush with the glaze while still hot.

VARIATION: To make buns, divide the dough into ten pieces, shape into rounds, leave to rise, then bake for about 15–20 minutes. Brush with the glaze while still hot.

Banana & Cardamom Bread

The combination of banana and cardamom is delicious in this soft-textured moist loaf. It is perfect for teatime, served with butter and jam.

Makes 1 loaf

INGREDIENTS
150 ml/¼ pint/⅔ cup warm water
5 ml/1 tsp dried yeast
pinch of sugar
10 cardamom pods
400 g/14 oz/3½ cups strong white
   bread flour
5 ml/1 tsp salt
30 ml/2 tbsp malt extract
2 ripe bananas, mashed
5 ml/1 tsp sesame seeds, to sprinkle

1 Put the water in a small bowl. Sprinkle the yeast on top, add the sugar and mix thoroughly. Leave for 10 minutes. Meanwhile, split the cardamom pods and remove the seeds. Chop the seeds finely.

2 Sift the flour and salt into a mixing bowl and make a well in the centre. Add the yeast mixture with the malt extract, chopped cardamom seeds and mashed bananas.

3 Gradually incorporate the flour and mix to a soft dough, adding a little extra water if necessary. Turn the dough on to a floured surface and knead for about 5 minutes, until smooth and elastic. Return to the clean bowl, cover and leave in a warm place to rise for about 2 hours.

4 Grease a baking sheet. Turn the dough on to a floured surface, knead briefly, then shape into a braid. Place the braid on the baking sheet, cover and leave to rise. Preheat the oven to 220°C/425°F/Gas 7.

5 Brush the braid lightly with water and sprinkle with the sesame seeds. Bake for 10 minutes, then lower the oven temperature to 200°C/400°F/Gas 6. Cook for 15 minutes more, or until the loaf is ready. Allow to cool on a wire rack.

Sultana & Walnut Bread

This bread is delicious with savoury or sweet toppings. Spread with butter or soft margarine and add salami, cheese, jam or honey.

Makes 1 loaf

INGREDIENTS
300 g/11 oz/2¾ cups strong white bread flour
2.5 ml/½ tsp salt
15 g/½ oz/1 tbsp butter
7.5 ml/1½ tsp easy-blend (rapid-rise)
    dried yeast
175 ml/6 fl oz/¾ cup lukewarm water
115 g/4 oz/scant 1 cup sultanas
    (golden raisins)
75 g/3 oz/½ cup walnuts, roughly chopped
melted butter, for brushing

1 Sift the flour and salt into a bowl, cut in the butter with a knife, then stir in the yeast.

2 Gradually add the lukewarm water, stirring with a spoon at first, then gathering the dough together with your hands.

3 Turn the dough out on to a floured surface. Knead for about 10 minutes, until smooth and elastic.

4 Knead the sultanas and walnuts into the dough until they are evenly distributed. Shape into an oval shape, place on a lightly oiled baking sheet, cover and leave in a warm place to rise for 1–2 hours. Preheat the oven to 220°C/425°F/Gas 7.

5 Uncover the loaf and bake for 10 minutes, then reduce the oven temperature to 190°C/375°F/Gas 5. Bake for a further 20–25 minutes.

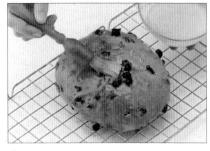

6 Transfer the loaf to a wire rack, brush with the melted butter and cover with a dishtowel. Allow the loaf to cool before slicing.

Barm Brack

It used to be traditional to bake a wedding ring in this Irish Hallowe'en bread as a marriage charm.

Makes 1 loaf

INGREDIENTS
675 g/1½ lb/6 cups plain (all-purpose) flour
2.5 ml/½ tsp mixed (apple pie) spice
5 ml/1 tsp salt
1 sachet easy-blend (rapid-rise)
    dried yeast
50 g/2 oz/¼ cup caster (superfine) sugar
300 ml/½ pint/1¼ cups
    lukewarm milk
150 ml/¼ pint/⅔ cup
    lukewarm water
50 g/2 oz/4 tbsp butter, softened
225 g/8 oz/1⅓ cups sultanas (golden raisins)
50 g/2 oz/⅓ cup currants
50 g/2 oz/⅓ cup chopped mixed
    (candied) peel
milk, for glazing

1 Sift the plain flour, mixed spice and salt into a large bowl. Stir in the dried yeast and 15 ml/1 tbsp of the caster sugar. Make a well in the centre and pour in the lukewarm milk and water.

2 Mix well, gradually incorporating the dry ingredients to make a sticky dough. Place on a lightly floured board and knead the dough until smooth and elastic. Put into a clean bowl. Cover and leave to rise for about 1 hour.

3 Knead the dough lightly on a floured surface. Add the remaining ingredients, apart from the milk for glazing, and work them in. Return the dough to the bowl, cover and leave to rise for 30 minutes.

4 Grease a 23 cm/9 in round cake tin (pan). Pat the dough to a neat round and fit it in the tin. Cover and leave to rise for about 45 minutes.

5 Preheat the oven to 200°C/400°F/ Gas 6. Brush the loaf lightly with milk and bake for 15 minutes. Cover the loaf with foil, reduce the oven temperature to 180°C/350°F/Gas 4 and bake for 45 minutes more, or until golden and ready. Cool on a wire rack.

Split Tin

As its name suggests, this popular and homely loaf is so called because of the distinctive centre split.

Makes 1 loaf

INGREDIENTS
500 g/1¼ lb/5 cups strong white bread flour, plus extra for dusting
10 ml/2 tsp salt
15 g/½ oz fresh yeast
300 ml/½ pint/1¼ cups lukewarm water
60 ml/4 tbsp lukewarm milk

1 Lightly grease a 900 g/2 lb loaf tin (pan). Sift the flour and salt into a bowl and make a well in the centre. Mix the yeast with the lukewarm water. Pour the yeast mixture into the well and mix in a little flour with your fingers. Gradually mix in more of the flour from around the edge of the bowl to form a thick, smooth batter.

2 Sprinkle a little more flour from around the edge of the bowl over the batter and leave in a warm place to sponge. Add the lukewarm milk and remaining flour; mix to a firm dough.

3 Knead on a lightly floured surface for about 10 minutes, until smooth and elastic. Place in a lightly oiled bowl, cover and leave in a warm place to rise for 1–1¼ hours.

4 Knock back (punch down) the dough and turn out on to a lightly floured surface. Shape it into a rectangle the length of the tin. Roll up lengthways, tuck the ends under and place seam side down in the tin. Cover and leave to rise for 20–30 minutes.

5 Using a sharp knife, make a deep slash along the length of the bread; dust with flour. Leave for 15 minutes.

6 Meanwhile, preheat the oven to 230°C/450°F/Gas 8. Bake for 15 minutes, then reduce the oven temperature to 200°C/400°F/Gas 6. Bake for 20–25 minutes more, or until the bread is golden and ready. Turn out on to a wire rack to cool.

COOK'S TIP: Another sure sign that the loaf is ready is that it will have shrunk slightly away from the sides of the tin (pan).

Country Bread

This traditional American loaf, made with a mixture of wholemeal and white flours, not only tastes delicious, but also looks wonderful.

Makes 2 loaves

INGREDIENTS
275 g/10 oz/2½ cups wholemeal
  (whole-wheat) flour, plus extra for dusting
275 g/10 oz/2½ cups plain (all-purpose) flour
115 g/4 oz/1 cup strong white
  bread flour
20 ml/4 tsp salt
50 g/2 oz/4 tbsp butter,
  at room temperature
475 ml/16 fl oz/2 cups lukewarm milk

FOR THE STARTER
1 sachet easy-blend (rapid-rise)
  dried yeast
250 ml/8 fl oz/1 cup lukewarm water
115 g/4 oz/1 cup plain (all-purpose) flour
1.5 ml/¼ tsp sugar

1 For the starter, stir together the yeast, water, flour and sugar. Cover and leave in a warm place for 2–3 hours or overnight in a cool place.

2 Place the flours, salt and butter in a food processor and process for 1–2 minutes, until just blended. Stir together the milk and starter, then slowly pour into the processor, with the motor running, until the mixture forms a dough. If necessary, add more water. Alternatively, mix the dough by hand. Transfer to a floured surface and knead until smooth and elastic.

3 Place in an ungreased bowl, cover and leave to rise for about 1½ hours.

4 Transfer to a floured surface and knead briefly. Return to the clean bowl and leave to rise for about 1½ hours.

5 Divide the dough in half. Cut off one-third of the dough from each half and shape into balls. Shape the larger remaining portion of each half into balls. Grease a baking sheet.

6 Top each large ball with a small one. Press the centre with the handle of a wooden spoon to secure. Slash the top, cover with a plastic bag and let rise.

7 Preheat the oven to 200°C/400°F/ Gas 6. Bake the dough, sprinkled with wholemeal flour, for 45–50 minutes, until browned. Cool on a rack.

165

Granary Cob

You can make this loaf plain, with a slash across the top for a Danish cob or with a cross cut in the top for a Coburg cob.

Makes 1 loaf

INGREDIENTS
450 g/1 lb/4 cups Granary (whole-wheat) flour
10 ml/2 tsp salt
15 g/½ oz fresh yeast
300 ml/½ pint/1¼ cups lukewarm water or milk and water mixed

FOR THE TOPPING
30 ml/2 tbsp water
2.5 ml/½ tsp salt
wheat flakes or cracked wheat

1 Lightly flour a baking sheet. Sift the flour and salt into a bowl and make a well in the centre. Place in a very low oven for 5 minutes to warm.

2 Mix the yeast with a little of the lukewarm water or milk mixture then blend in the rest. Add the yeast mixture to the centre of the warmed Granary flour and mix well to form a dough.

3 Turn the dough out on to a lightly floured surface and knead for about 10 minutes, until smooth and elastic. Place in a lightly oiled bowl, cover and leave in a warm place to rise for 1¼ hours.

4 Turn the dough out on to a lightly floured surface and knock back (punch down). Knead for 2–3 minutes, then roll into a ball. Place on the prepared baking sheet. Cover with an inverted bowl and leave to rise again for 30–45 minutes.

5 For the topping, mix the water and salt and brush over the bread. Sprinkle the surface with wheat flakes or cracked wheat. Preheat the oven to 230°C/450°F/Gas 8.

6 Bake the Granary loaf for 15 minutes, then reduce the oven temperature to 200°C/400°F/Gas 6 and bake for 20 minutes more, or until the loaf is ready. Leave to cool on a wire rack.

Jams, Jellies and Preserves

Strawberry Jam

Capture the essence of summer in a jar of home-made strawberry jam – a favourite with old and young alike.

Makes about 1.5 kg/3 lb

INGREDIENTS
1 kg/2¼ lb/8 cups small strawberries
900 g/2 lb/4½ cups
   granulated sugar
juice of 2 lemons
scones and clotted cream,
   to serve (optional)

2 The next day, scrape the fruit and juice into a large, heavy pan. Add the lemon juice. Gradually bring to the boil over a low heat, stirring until the sugar has dissolved.

1 Place the strawberries in layers in a large bowl, sprinkling each layer with sugar. Cover and leave overnight.

3 Boil steadily for 10–15 minutes, or until the jam reaches setting point. Cool for 10 minutes.

COOK'S TIPS: For best results, don't wash the strawberries. Instead, brush off any dirt, or wipe the strawberries with a damp cloth. If you have to wash any, pat them dry and then spread them out on a clean dishtowel to dry further. This jam can be stored in a cool, dark place for up to 1 year.

4 Pour the jam into warm sterilized jars, filling them right to the top. Cover and seal the jars while hot and label when cold. Serve the jam with scones and clotted cream, if you like.

Rhubarb & Ginger Mint Jam

Ginger mint is easily grown in the garden, and is just the thing to boost the flavour of rhubarb jam.

Makes about 2.75 kg/6 lb

INGREDIENTS
2 kg/4½ lb rhubarb, trimmed
250 ml/8 fl oz/1 cup water
juice of 1 lemon
5 cm/2 in piece fresh root
  ginger
1.5 kg/3 lb/6¾ cups sugar
115 g/4 oz/⅔ cup stem
  ginger, chopped
30–45 ml/2–3 tbsp very finely chopped
  ginger mint leaves

1 Cut the rhubarb into 2.5 cm/1 in pieces. Place the rhubarb, water and lemon juice in a large, heavy pan and bring to the boil.

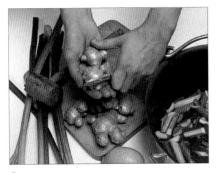

2 Peel and bruise the root ginger and add it to the pan. Simmer, stirring frequently, until the rhubarb is soft, then remove the ginger.

3 Add the sugar and stir until it has dissolved. Bring the mixture to the boil and boil rapidly for 10–15 minutes, or until setting point is reached. With a metal slotted spoon, remove any scum from the surface.

4 Add the stem ginger and ginger mint leaves. Pour into warm, sterilized jars, cover and seal while the jam is hot and label when cold.

VARIATION: If ginger mint is not available you can substitute garden or apple mint. Avoid peppermint or Moroccan mint as these are more suitable for making mint tea.

COOK'S TIP: The early, forced rhubarb has the finest flavour.

Melon & Star Anise Jam

Melon and ginger are classic companions. The addition of star anise imparts a wonderful aromatic flavour to the jam.

Makes 450 g/1 lb

INGREDIENTS

2 charentais or cantaloupe melons,
　peeled and seeded
450 g/1 lb/2¼ cups granulated sugar
2 star anise
4 pieces stem ginger in syrup, drained and
　finely chopped
finely grated rind and juice of
　2 lemons

1 Dice the melons and layer with the granulated sugar in a large non-metallic bowl. Cover with clear film (plastic wrap) and leave overnight so the melons can release their juices.

COOK'S TIP: The large amount of sugar is necessary for proper jelling. Use this jam in savoury dishes instead of honey to add a spicy, non-cloying sweetness.

2 Pour the marinated melons and their juice into a large, heavy pan and add the star anise, chopped stem ginger, finely grated lemon rind and juice.

3 Bring to the boil over a medium heat, stirring to ensure that all the sugar has dissolved, then lower the heat. Simmer for 25 minutes, or until the melon has become transparent and the setting point has been reached. If preferred, remove the star anise, using a slotted spoon.

4 Spoon the jam into warm, sterilized jars. Cover the fruit with liquid and seal while it is hot and label when cold. It will keep for several months in a cool, dark cupboard. Once a jar has been opened, the jam should be stored in the refrigerator and used within 2 weeks.

Dried Apricot Jam

Make this jam when reserves look low in winter.

Makes about 2 kg/4½ lb

INGREDIENTS
675 g/1½ lb dried apricots
900 ml/1½ pints/3¾ cups apple juice made
   with concentrate
juice and rind of 2 lemons
675 g/1½ lb/3½ cups preserving sugar
50 g/2 oz/⅓ cup blanched almonds,
   coarsely chopped

1 Put the apricots in a large bowl
and add the apple juice. Set aside to
soak overnight.

2 Pour the apricots and juice into a
pan and add the lemon juice and rind.
Bring to the boil, lower the heat and
simmer for 15–20 minutes.

3 Meanwhile, warm the sugar in a
low oven. Add the warm sugar to the
apricots and bring back to the boil,
stirring constantly until the sugar has
completely dissolved. Boil until setting
point is reached.

4 Stir in the chopped almonds and set
aside for 15 minutes. Pour the apricot
jam into warm, sterilized jars. Cover
and seal while the jam is hot and label
when cold.

VARIATION: This recipe would
also work well using dried peaches
instead of the apricots.

Clementine Marmalade

Coriander seeds impart a warm and spicy flavour to this marmalade.

Makes about 2.75 kg/6 lb

INGREDIENTS

1.5 kg/3 lb clementines
6 lemons
30 ml/2 tbsp coriander seeds, roasted and
  roughly crushed
3 litres/5¼ pints/12 cups water
1.5 kg/3 lb/6¾ cups
  preserving sugar

1 Cut the clementines and lemons in half. Squeeze all the fruit and pour the juice into a large, heavy pan.

2 Scrape the pith from the citrus shells and tie it, with the pips (seeds) and half the coriander, in muslin (cheesecloth). Add the bag to the juice.

3 Slice the clementine and lemon peels into fine shreds and add them to the pan with the water.

4 Bring the water to the boil, lower the heat and simmer for 1½ hours or until the peel is very soft. Remove the muslin bag. Holding it over the pan, squeeze it between two saucers.

5 Add the sugar and the remaining coriander to the pan and stir over a low heat until dissolved. Boil rapidly until setting point is reached. Skim the surface, then leave to stand for 30 minutes, stirring occasionally. Pour into warm, sterilized jars, cover and seal while the marmalade is hot and label when cold.

Three-fruit Marmalade

This zesty marmalade is incomparably better than store-bought varieties.

Makes 2.75 kg/6 lb

INGREDIENTS
350 g/12 oz oranges
350 g/12 oz lemons
675 g/1½ lb grapefruit
2.5 litres/4½ pints/10 cups water
2.75 kg/6 lb/14 cups granulated sugar

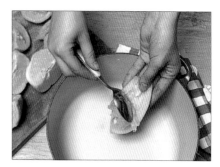

3 Remove the fruit from the pan and cut it into quarters. Scrape out the pulp and add it to the pan with the cooking liquid.

1 Remove any labels from the oranges, lemons and grapefruit, then rinse and gently scrub the fruit with a vegetable brush.

2 Put all the fruit and water in a large, heavy pan. Ensure that the water covers the fruit. Bring to the boil then simmer, uncovered, for 2 hours. Leave in the pan until the fruit is cool enough to be handled.

VARIATION: You can adjust the amount of orange or lemon in this recipe, keeping the same total weight, to produce a sweeter or tarter flavour.

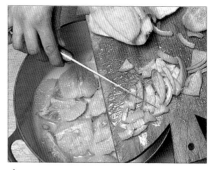

4 Cut the rinds into slivers and add to the pan. Add the sugar. Gently heat until the sugar has dissolved. Bring to the boil and cook until a setting point is reached. Leave to stand for 1 hour to allow the peel to settle. Pour into warm, sterilized jars, cover and seal while the marmalade is hot and label when cold.

Lemon & Lime Curd

Serve this creamy, tangy spread with toast or muffins, instead of jam, for a delightful change of flavour and texture.

Makes 900 g/2 lb

INGREDIENTS
115 g/4 oz/½ cup unsalted (sweet) butter
3 eggs
2 lemons and 2 limes
225 g/8 oz/generous 1 cup caster
  (superfine) sugar

1 Put the butter in a mixing bowl placed over a pan of simmering water, but not touching the surface.

2 Lightly beat the eggs with a fork and add them to the butter.

3 Finely grate the rinds of the lemons and limes, then cut them in half and squeeze the juice. Add the lemon and lime rinds and juices to the eggs and butter, then add the sugar.

4 Stir the mixture constantly until it thickens. Pour into small, warm sterilized jars. Cover and seal while the curd is hot and label when cold. The lemon and lime curd will keep unopened for up to a month. Once opened, keep in the refrigerator and consume within a week.

Bramble Jelly

This jelly has to be made with hand-picked wild blackberries for the best flavour. Include a few red, unripe berries for a good set.

Makes 900 g/2 lb

INGREDIENTS
900 g/2 lb/8 cups blackberries
300 ml/½ pint/1¼ cups water
juice of 1 lemon
about 900 g/2 lb/4½ cups caster
   (superfine) sugar
hot buttered toast or English muffins,
   to serve

1 Put the blackberries, water and lemon juice into a large, heavy pan. Cover the pan and cook over a gentle heat for 15–30 minutes, or until the blackberries are very soft.

2 Ladle into a jelly bag or a large sieve (strainer) lined with muslin (cheesecloth) and set over a large bowl. Leave to drip overnight to obtain the maximum amount of juice. Do not squeeze the bag as this will make the jelly cloudy.

3 Discard the fruit pulp. Measure the juice and allow 450 g/1 lb/2¼ cups sugar to every 600 ml/1 pint/ 2½ cups juice. Place the sugar and blackberry juice in a large, heavy pan and bring the mixture slowly to the boil, stirring constantly until the sugar has dissolved.

4 Boil rapidly until setting point is reached. This will take about 10 minutes. Cool for 10 minutes. Skim off any scum and pour the jelly into warm, sterilized jars. Cover and seal while the jelly is hot and label when cold. Serve the jelly with hot buttered toast or muffins.

VARIATION: Redcurrant jelly is made in the same way, but with less sugar. Reduce the quantity to 350 g/12 oz/1⅔ cups for every 600 ml/1 pint/2½ cups juice.

Crab Apple & Lavender Jelly

This delicate, clear jelly with its fragrance of summer looks even prettier with a sprig of fresh lavender suspended in the jar.

Makes about 900 g/2 lb

INGREDIENTS
900 g/2 lb/5 cups crab apples
1.75 litres/3 pints/7½ cups water
lavender stems
900 g/2 lb/4½ cups
    granulated sugar

1 Cut the unpeeled crab apples into chunks and place in a large, heavy pan with the water and 2 stems of lavender. Bring to the boil, cover and simmer very gently, stirring occasionally, for 1 hour, until the fruit is pulpy.

2 Pour the apple mixture into a large jelly bag or a sieve (strainer) lined with muslin (cheesecloth) and set over a large bowl. Leave to drain for several hours or overnight. Do not squeeze the bag or the jelly will become cloudy.

3 Discard the crab apple pulp and measure the quantity of juice in the bowl. To each 600 ml/1 pint/2½ cups of juice add 450 g/1 lb/2¼ cups granulated sugar. Put the measured sugar and juice into a clean pan.

4 Heat the juice gently, stirring occasionally, until the sugar has dissolved. Bring to the boil and boil rapidly for about 8–10 minutes, until setting point has been reached. Remove the pan from the heat.

5 Skim the jelly with a slotted spoon. Ladle it into warm, sterilized jars. Dip the lavender stems quickly into boiling water, gently shake off the excess water, then insert a stem into each jar. Cover and seal while the jelly is hot and label the jars when cold.

Crab Apple Jelly

Serve this jelly with scones or use it to glaze an apple tart.

Makes about 1 kg/2¼ lb from each 600 ml/1 pint/ 2½ cups liquid

INGREDIENTS
1 kg/2¼ lb/5⅔ cups crab apples
3 cloves
about 900 g/2 lb/4½ cups preserving sugar

1 Wash the apples and halve them, but do not peel or core. Place the apples and cloves in a large, heavy pan and cover with water. Bring to the boil, lower the heat and simmer until soft.

2 Ladle into a large jelly bag or a sieve (strainer) lined with muslin (cheesecloth) and set over a large bowl. Leave to drain.

3 Warm the sugar in a low oven (120°C/250°F/Gas ½) for 15 minutes. Measure the juice and discard the fruit. Allow 450 g/1 lb/2¼ cups sugar for each 600 ml/1 pint/2½ cups of juice.

4 Put the juice and sugar in a large, heavy pan. Heat gently, stirring until the sugar dissolves, then boil rapidly until setting point is reached. Pour into warm, sterilized jars, cover and seal while the jelly is still hot and label when cold.

Rosehip & Apple Jelly

You can use windfall apples and rosehips from the hedgerows.

Makes about 1 kg/2¼ lb from each 600 ml/1 pint/ 2½ cups liquid

INGREDIENTS
1 kg/2¼ lb cooking apples, peeled, trimmed and quartered
450 g/1 lb firm, ripe rosehips
preserving sugar

1 Put the apples in a large, heavy pan with just enough water to cover, plus 300 ml/½ pint/1¼ cups extra. Bring to the boil and cook the apples until they are a pulp. Coarsely chop the rosehips in a food processor. Add them to the pan and simmer for 10 minutes.

2 Leave to stand for 10 minutes, then ladle into a jelly bag or sieve (strainer) lined with muslin (cheesecloth) and set over a bowl. Leave to drain overnight.

3 Measure the juice and discard the fruit. Allow 400 g/14 oz/2 cups sugar for each 600 ml/1 pint/2½ cups of liquid. Warm the sugar in a low oven. Bring the juice to the boil in a large, heavy pan and add the sugar. Stir until it has dissolved, then boil until setting point is reached. Pour into warm, sterilized jars, cover and seal while the jelly is still hot and label when cold.

Rose Petal Jelly

This subtle jelly is ideal for traditional afternoon teas with thinly sliced bread and butter – it adds a real summer flavour.

Makes about 900 g/2 lb

INGREDIENTS
600 ml/1 pint/2½ cups red or
   pink roses
450 ml/¾ pint/scant 2 cups water
700 g/1 lb 9 oz/3½ cups caster
   (superfine) sugar
100 ml/3½ fl oz/scant ½ cup white
   grape juice
100 ml/3½ fl oz/scant ½ cup red
   grape juice
50 g/2 oz packet powdered
   fruit pectin
30 ml/2 tbsp rosewater

2 Strain the flowers from the syrup, and put the syrup in a large, heavy pan. Add the grape juices and pectin. Boil hard for 1 minute.

3 Add the remaining sugar and stir well. Boil the mixture hard for 1 minute more. Remove from the heat. Test for setting point – it should make a soft jelly, not a thick jam.

4 Finally, add the rosewater. Ladle the jelly into warm, sterilized jars, cover and seal while the jelly is hot and label when cold.

1 Carefully pull the rose petals away from the flower and trim them at the base to remove the white tips. Place the petals, water and about one-eighth of the sugar in a pan and bring to the boil. Reduce the heat and simmer for 5 minutes. Remove from the heat and leave to stand overnight for the rose fragrance to infuse.

COOK'S TIP: Powdered pectin is needed here because the jelly does not include fruit which contains its own pectin.

Jellies should be bright and clear and not too firmly set.

Mint & Apple Jelly

Makes 4 small jars

INGREDIENTS
1.5 kg/3 lb cooking apples
150 ml/¼ pint/⅔ cup cider vinegar
750 ml/1¼ pints/3 cups water
500–675 g/1¼–1½ lb/3–3½ cups
   granulated sugar
60 ml/4 tbsp chopped fresh mint
few drops green food colouring (optional)

1 Roughly chop the apples, including cores and skin, and put into a large, heavy pan. Add the vinegar and water and bring to the boil. Reduce the heat and simmer for 30 minutes, or until the apples are pulpy.

2 Ladle the apple mixture into a jelly bag or sieve (strainer) lined with muslin (cheesecloth) and set over a bowl. Drain for several hours.

3 Measure the juice and pour back into the pan. For each 600 ml/1 pint/ 2½ cups of juice, add 450 g/1 lb/ 2¼ cups sugar. Boil until the sugar has completely dissolved.

4 Boil rapidly for 10–15 minutes, or until setting point is reached. Skim with a slotted spoon. Stir in the mint and food colouring, if liked. Ladle into warm, sterilized jars, cover and seal while hot.

Apple & Strawberry Jelly

This delicious jelly can be served with scones or home-made bread.

Makes 5 medium-sized jars

INGREDIENTS
900 g/2 lb cooking apples
1.2 litres/2 pints/5 cups water
900 g/2 lb strawberries
1 kg/2¼ lb/generous 5 cups
    granulated sugar
5 stems rosemary

1 Chop the apples, including cores and skin, and put in a large heavy pan with the water. Bring to the boil and simmer for 15 minutes. Thickly slice the strawberries, add them to the pan, bring back to the boil and simmer for 15 minutes.

2 Ladle the fruit mixture into a large jelly bag or a sieve (strainer) lined with muslin (cheesecloth) and set over a large bowl. Leave to drain for several hours or overnight.

3 Measure the juice and add 450 g/1 lb/2¼ cups sugar to every 600 ml/1 pint/2½ cups juice. Dissolve the sugar slowly then boil rapidly until setting point is reached.

4 Skim the jelly with a slotted spoon. Ladle it into warm, sterilized jars and leave to stand for 10 minutes. Add a sprig of rosemary to each jar, cover and seal. Label the jars when cold.

Red Pepper & Rosemary Jelly

This wonderful amber-coloured jelly may be made with either red or yellow peppers and flavoured with any full-flavoured herbs.

Makes 1.75 kg/4 lb

INGREDIENTS
450 g/1 lb/8 tomatoes, quartered
4 red (bell) peppers, seeded and chopped
2 red chillies, seeded and chopped
rosemary sprigs, blanched in boiling water
300 ml/½ pint/1¼ cups water
300 ml/½ pint/1¼ cups red wine vinegar
2.5 ml/½ tsp salt
900 g/2 lb/4½ cups preserving sugar
250 ml/8 fl oz/1 cup liquid pectin

3 Place the juice in a clean pan with the vinegar, salt and sugar. Heat gently, stirring occasionally, until the sugar has dissolved. Boil rapidly for 3 minutes.

4 Remove the pan from the heat and stir in the liquid pectin. Skim the surface with a piece of kitchen paper to remove any foam.

1 Place the tomatoes, peppers, chillies, a few rosemary sprigs and the water into a large, heavy pan and bring to the boil. Cover and simmer for 1 hour, or until the peppers are tender and pulpy.

2 Ladle the mixture into a large jelly bag or a sieve (strainer) lined with muslin (cheesecloth) and set over a large bowl. Leave to drain for several hours or, preferably, overnight.

5 Pour the liquid into warm, sterilized jars and add a sprig of rosemary to each jar. Cover and seal while hot and label when cold.

Fruits in Liqueur

Choose from apricots, clementines, kumquats, physalis, cherries, strawberries, raspberries, peaches, plums, star fruit or seedless grapes and team them with rum, brandy, kirsch or Cointreau.

Makes 450 g/1 lb

INGREDIENTS
450 g/1 lb/3 cups fresh fruit
225 g/8 oz/generous 1 cup
    granulated sugar
300 ml/½ pint/1¼ cups water
150 ml/¼ pint/⅔ cup liqueur or spirit

1 Wash the fruit. Halve and stone apricots, plums or peaches. Slice star fruit, remove the husk from physalis, hull strawberries or raspberries, and prick kumquats, cherries or grapes all over with a cocktail stick. Pare the rind from clementines using a sharp knife, taking care not to include any white pith.

2 Place 115 g/4 oz/scant ½ cup of the sugar and the water into a pan. Heat gently, stirring occasionally, until the sugar has dissolved. Bring to the boil.

3 Add the fruit and simmer gently for 1–2 minutes, until the fruit is just tender, but the skins are intact and the fruits are whole.

4 Carefully remove the fruit using a slotted spoon and arrange neatly in warm, sterilized jars. Add the remaining sugar to the syrup in the pan and stir until dissolved.

5 Boil the syrup rapidly until it reaches 107°C/225°F or the thread stage. Test by pressing a small amount of syrup between 2 teaspoons; when they are pulled apart, a thread should form. Allow to cool.

6 Measure the cooled syrup, then add an equal quantity of liqueur or spirit. Mix until blended. Pour over the fruit until covered. Seal each jar and keep for up to 4 months.

Fruit Preserves

The time to make these luxurious preserves is in high summer when the fruit is at its cheapest and most flavoursome. They are delicious served with cream or ice cream.

Brandied Peaches

Makes 1.75 kg/4 lb peaches, plus syrup

INGREDIENTS
1.75 kg/4 lb/10¼ cups granulated sugar
600 ml/1 pint/2½ cups water
2 cinnamon sticks, broken
15 ml/1 tbsp cloves
1.75 kg/4 lb ripe but firm peaches, scalded
    and peeled
400 ml/14 fl oz/1⅔ cups brandy

1 Dissolve the sugar in the water in a pan over a gentle heat. Tie the cinnamon sticks and cloves in a piece of muslin and add them to the sugar water. Bring to the boil.

2 Add the peaches, a few at a time, and simmer each batch for about 5 minutes, until just tender. Drain the cooked peaches, pouring the syrup back into the pan. When all the peaches are cooked, boil the syrup until it has thickened slightly. Cool for 10 minutes.

3 Stir the brandy into the syrup. Pack the peaches into hot, sterilized bottles, cover with the syrup and seal.

Cherries in Eau-de-vie

Makes 450 g/1 lb cherries, plus syrup

INGREDIENTS
450 g/1 lb/2⅔ cups ripe cherries
8 blanched almonds
90 ml/6 tbsp
    granulated sugar
550 ml/18 fl oz/2½ cups
    eau-de-vie

1 Wash and pit the cherries and then pack them, together with the blanched almonds, into a sterilized, wide-necked bottle.

2 Spoon the sugar over the cherries and almonds, then add the eau-de-vie so that the cherries are just covered. Seal the top securely.

3 Store in a cool, dark place for 1 month before using the cherries, shaking the bottle from time to time to help dissolve the sugar.

COOK'S TIP: Whole, preserved cherries can also be dipped in melted chocolate.

Poached Spiced Plums in Brandy

Makes 900 g/2 lb

INGREDIENTS
600 ml/1 pint/2½ cups brandy
rind of 1 lemon, peeled in a long strip
350 g/12 oz/1⅔ cups caster (superfine) sugar
1 cinnamon stick
900 g/2 lb fresh plums

1 Put the brandy, lemon rind, sugar and cinnamon stick in a large pan and heat gently to dissolve the sugar. Add the plums and poach for about 15 minutes, or until soft. Remove with a slotted spoon.

2 Reduce the syrup by a third by rapid boiling. Strain it over the plums. Bottle the plums in large sterilized jars. Seal tightly and store for up to 6 months in a cool, dark place.

COOK'S TIP: This recipe would also work well with golden plums or damsons. For an extra fruity flavour, you could use plum brandy, quetsch or prunella, and mirabelle would be ideal for golden plums.

Above: Poached Spiced Plums in Brandy

197

Raspberry Preserve

The wonderfully fresh flavour of this fruit preserve turns a home-made scone or teabread into a delicious treat.

Makes 900 g/2 lb

INGREDIENTS
675 g/1½ lb/4 cups raspberries
900 g/2 lb/4½ cups caster
   (superfine) sugar
30 ml/2 tbsp lemon juice
120 ml/4 fl oz/½ cup
   liquid pectin

1 Place the raspberries in a large bowl and lightly crush with a wooden spoon. Stir in the caster sugar. Leave for 1 hour at room temperature, stirring occasionally.

2 Add the lemon juice and pectin to the raspberries and stir until thoroughly blended.

3 Spoon the raspberry mixture into sterilized jars, leaving a 1 cm/½ in space at the top if the jam is to be frozen. Cover the surface of each with a baking parchment disc and seal with a lid or cellophane paper and a rubber band. Do not use a screw-topped lid if the jam is to be frozen. Label and freeze for up to 6 months, or refrigerate for up to 4 weeks.

Traditional Mincemeat

Mince pies are an essential part of the traditional Christmas fare, enjoyed in considerable quantities throughout the holiday.

Makes about 1.75 g/4 lb

INGREDIENTS

450 g/1 lb cooking apples
225 g/8 oz/1½ cups candied citrus peel
225 g/8 oz/1 cup currants
225 g/8 oz/1⅓ cups sultanas (golden raisins)
450 g/1 lb/3¼ cups seedless raisins
115 g/4 oz/⅔ cup blanched almonds, chopped
225 g/8 oz/1⅔ cup suet or vegetarian suet
225 g/8 oz/1 cup soft dark brown sugar
5 ml/1 tsp ground cinnamon
5 ml/1 tsp ground allspice
5 ml/1 tsp ground ginger
2.5 ml/½ tsp grated nutmeg
grated rind and juice of 2 oranges
grated rind and juice of 2 lemons
about 150 ml/¼ pint/⅔ cup brandy or port

1 Peel, core and chop the cooking apples. Chop the candied citrus peel.

2 Place all the ingredients, except the brandy or port, in a large mixing bowl. Stir well.

3 Cover the bowl with a cloth and set aside in a cool place overnight for the fruit to swell.

4 The following day, stir in enough brandy or port to make a mixture moist enough to drop from a spoon.

5 Spoon the mixture into sterilized jars and cover and store in a cool, dry place.

Candied Citrus Slices

To preserve the individual flavour of each citrus fruit they should all be candied separately.

Makes about 675 g/1½ lb

INGREDIENTS
5 large oranges or 10 lemons
  or 10 limes
675 g/1½ lb/3½ cups granulated sugar,
  plus extra for sprinkling
250 ml/8 fl oz/1 cup cold water

1 Halve the fruit, squeeze out the juice and discard the flesh, but retain the pith.

2 Cut the peel into strips about 1 cm/½ in wide and place them in a pan. Cover with boiling water and simmer for 5 minutes. Drain and then repeat this process 4 times, using fresh boiling water each time, to remove the peel's bitterness.

3 Put the sugar in a heavy pan and pour in the cold water. Heat gently to dissolve the sugar. Add the peel, partially cover and simmer over a low heat for 30–40 minutes, until soft. Leave to cool completely, then sprinkle with sugar to thoroughly cover the peel. Store the candied peel in an airtight container for up to 1 year.

Right: Candied Citrus Slices

Candied Ginger

You can use candied ginger in your cakes and cookies or simply nibble a piece as a treat.

Makes about 675 g/1½ lb

INGREDIENTS
350 g/12 oz fresh root ginger
225 g/8 oz/generous 1 cup granulated sugar
120 ml/4 fl oz/½ cup water
caster (superfine) sugar, for coating

1 Place the ginger in a pan and cover with water. Bring to the boil and simmer for 15 minutes. Drain and leave to cool. Peel the ginger and cut it into 5 mm/¼ in slices.

2 Place the sugar and water in a heavy pan. Heat gently until the sugar has dissolved, then simmer without stirring, for 15 minutes or until the mixture is syrupy.

3 Add the ginger and cook over a low heat, shaking the pan occasionally until the syrup has been absorbed. Remove the ginger slices from the pan and place them on a wire rack to cool.

4 Coat the slices with caster sugar and spread them out on baking parchment for 2–3 days, until the sugar has crystallized. Stored in an airtight jar, they will keep indefinitely.

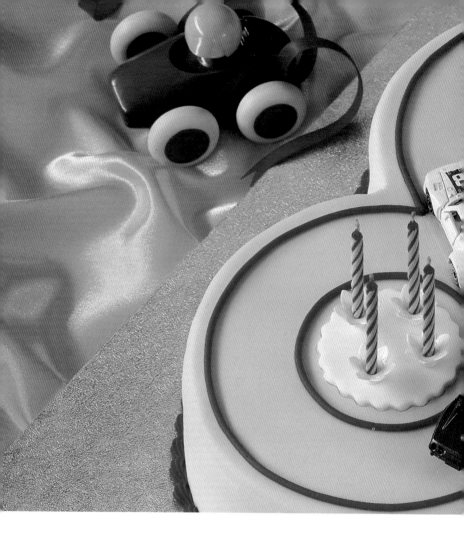

Party Cakes

A home-made cake is a lovely way to
show that you care, and there is
nothing so special as one designed
uniquely for the occasion. A novelty
cake is a wonderful way to celebrate a
family occasion, whether it is to wish
someone "bon voyage", or to celebrate
an engagement. Birthdays always need
a special cake, whether you are eight

or eighty. Who wouldn't appreciate a
Birthday Bowl of Strawberries or a
Flickering Candle Cake? And for the
kids there are party cakes shaped like
animals, a mermaid, a train and even a
computer game. Each cake is highly
distinctive, but not too difficult to
achieve. All are made from basic cake
recipes, icings and glazes, and step-by-

step instructions for these are included
in the first chapter of this book. You
can follow the recipes exactly or
adapt the designs to suit your own
family events. Whether you want to
celebrate a birthday, Christmas,
Mother's Day, or simply say "thank
you", do it in style with a special
home-made cake.

NOVELTY
CAKES

The Beautiful Present Cake

For a best friend, mother, grandmother, aunt or sister, this beautiful cake can mark any special occasion.

Serves 15–20

INGREDIENTS
2 x quantity quick-mix sponge cake, baked
 in a 23 cm/9 in square cake tin (pan)
1 quantity butter icing
60 ml/4 tbsp apricot glaze
1¼ x quantity marzipan
1⅔ x quantity sugarpaste (fondant) icing
purple and pink food colouring and pen

1 Cut the cake in half horizontally. Sandwich together with butter icing, place on a cake board and brush with apricot glaze. On a surface dusted with icing (confectioners') sugar roll out the marzipan to about 5 mm/¼ in thick and use to cover the cake.

2 Colour about five-eights of the sugarpaste purple. Roll out on a lightly dusted surface and use to cover the cake. With a heart-shaped cookie cutter, stamp out hearts, remove them with a knife, knead the trimmings and reserve wrapped in clear film (plastic wrap).

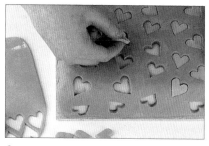

3 Colour the remaining icing pink and roll out to a 5 mm/¼ in thickness. Cut out hearts to fill the spaces. Wrap the trimmings and reserve.

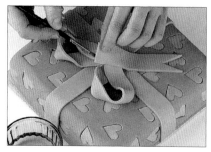

4 Roll out the pink icing and cut into three strips 2 cm/¾ in wide and 30 cm/12 in long. Lay two at right angles across the centre of cake, brushing with a little water to secure. Reserve the trimmings. Divide the remaining strip into quarters and arrange in the centre of the cake to make a bow. Secure with a little water and reserve the trimmings.

5 Roll out all the remaining icing and cut two rounds of each colour with a small fluted cutter. Roll the edges with a cocktail stick (toothpick) to make frilled petals. Make two small purple balls for flower centres. Assemble the flowers and secure to the cake with a little water. Make a name tag from the trimmings. Write a name with a food-colouring pen and secure to the cake.

Terracotta Flowerpot

Ideal for celebrating a gardener's birthday or Mother's Day, this flowerpot cake is filled with a colourful arrangement of icing flowers and foliage.

Serves 15

INGREDIENTS
1 x quantity Madeira cake, baked in a
    1.2 litre/2 pint/5 cup pudding bowl
175 g/6 oz/generous ½ cup jam
½ x quantity butter icing
30 ml/2 tbsp apricot glaze
2 x quantity sugarpaste (fondant) icing
orange-red, red, silver, green, purple and
    yellow food colouring
2 chocolate flakes, crushed
2 x quantity royal icing

1 Slice the cake into three layers and stick together with jam and butter icing. Cut out a shallow circle from the cake top, leaving a 1 cm/½ in rim.

2 Brush the outside of the cake and rim with apricot glaze. Tint 400 g/ 14 oz/2½ cups of the sugarpaste dark orange-red and cover the cake and rim. Reserve the trimmings. Leave to dry.

3 Use the trimmings to make decorations and handles for the flowerpot. Leave to dry on baking parchment before attaching using a little water. Sprinkle the chocolate flakes into the pot for soil.

4 Tint a small piece of sugarpaste very pale orange-red. Use to make a seed bag. When dry, paint on a pattern in food colouring. Tint two small pieces of icing red and silver. Make a trowel and leave to dry over a wooden spoon handle.

5 Tint the remaining icing green, purple and a small piece yellow. Use to make the flowers and leaves, attaching together with royal icing. Score leaf veins with the back of a knife. Make grass and seeds from trimmings. Leave to dry on baking parchment.

6 Place the leaves and flowers in the flowerpot with the seed bag, trowel, seeds and grass arranged around it.

Sun Cake

Whatever the star sign of the month, this cheerful sun cake would be a bright way to celebrate anyone's birthday.

Serves 10–12

INGREDIENTS

2 x quantity quick-mix sponge cake,
    baked in 2 x 15 cm/6 in round tins (pans)
25 g/1 oz/2 tbsp unsalted (sweet) butter
450 g/1 lb/4 cups sifted icing
    (confectiones') sugar
120 ml/4 fl oz/½ cup apricot glaze
2 large egg whites
1–2 drops glycerine
juice of 1 lemon
30 ml/2 tbsp water
yellow and orange
    food colouring

2 Brush the warm apricot glaze over the cake.

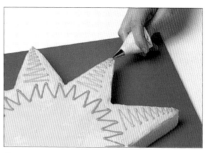

3 For the icing, beat the egg whites until stiff. Gradually add the icing sugar, glycerine and lemon juice, and beat for 1 minute. Reserve a small amount of icing for decoration, then tint the remainder yellow and spread over the cake. Tint the reserved icing bright yellow and orange. Pipe the details on to the cake.

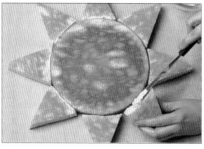

1 For the sunbeams cut one of the cakes into eight equal wedges. Cut away a rounded piece from the base of each so that they fit neatly up against the sides of the whole cake. Make butter icing with the butter and 25 g/1 oz/2 tbsp of the icing sugar. Place the whole cake on a 40 cm/ 16 in board and attach the sunbeams with the butter icing.

COOK'S TIP: If necessary, thin the icing with water or add icing (confectioners') sugar to thicken.

A Basket of Strawberries

Quick and easy to make, a perfect surprise for a birthday. Don't be put off by the icing technique, it's much easier than it looks!

Serves 6–8

INGREDIENTS

1 x quantity quick-mix sponge cake,
    baked in a 450 g/1 lb loaf tin (pan)
45 ml/3 tbsp apricot glaze
1½ x quantity marzipan
1 x quantity chocolate-flavour
    butter icing
red food colouring
50 g/2 oz/¼ cup caster (superfine) sugar
10 plastic strawberry stalks
30 cm/12 in thin red ribbon

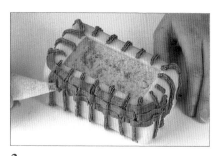

1 Level the top of the cake and make it perfectly flat. Score a 5 mm/¼ in border around the edge and scoop out the inside to make a shallow hollow. Brush the sides and border edges of the cake with apricot glaze.

2 Roll out 275 g/10 oz/scant 2 cups of the marzipan, cut into rectangles and use to cover the sides of the cake, overlapping the borders. Press the edges together to seal.

3 Using a basketweave nozzle, pipe vertical lines of chocolate-flavour butter icing 2.5 cm/1 in apart all around the sides of the cake. Pipe short horizontal lines alternately crossing over and then stopping at the vertical lines to give a basketweave effect. Using a star nozzle, pipe a decorative line of icing around the top edge of the basket to finish.

4 Tint the remaining marzipan red and mould it into ten strawberry shapes. Roll the shapes in the caster sugar and press a plastic stalk into each top. Carefully arrange the strawberries in the "basket".

5 For the basket handle, fold 30 x 7.5 cm/12 x 3 in strip of foil into a thin strip and wind the ribbon around it to cover. Bend up the ends and then bend into a curve. Push the ends into the sides of the cake. Decorate with bows made from ribbon.

The Beehive

The perfect cake for an outdoors spring or summer party. Take the bees along separately on their wires and insert them into the cake at the picnic.

Serves 8–10

INGREDIENTS
2 x quantity marzipan
icing (confectioners') sugar, for dusting
1 x quantity quick-mix sponge cake, baked
  in a 900 ml/1½ pint/3¾ cup pudding bowl
75 ml/5 tbsp apricot glaze
black food colouring
20 cm/8 in square of rice paper
25 g/1 oz sugarpaste (fondant) icing
florist's wire covered in florist's tape

1 Cut off about 175 g/6 oz of marzipan and set aside, wrapped in clear film (plastic wrap). Knead the remainder on a surface lightly dusted with icing sugar, then roll into a long, thin sausage shape. If it breaks, make more than one sausage. Place the cake, dome side up, on a cake board and brush with apricot glaze.

2 Starting at the back of the base, coil the marzipan sausage around the cake. Place any joins at the back.

3 With a small, sharp knife, cut an arched doorway at the front. Remove the cut-out section and cut away some of the cake to make a hollow.

4 To make six bees, halve the reserved marzipan and colour one half black. Set aside a cherry-sized ball of black marzipan, wrapped in clear film.

5 Divide the remaining marzipan into 12 small balls in each colour. To make a bee, pinch together two balls of each colour, alternately placed. Secure with a little water, if necessary. Cut the rice paper into six pairs of wings and stick to the bees with water.

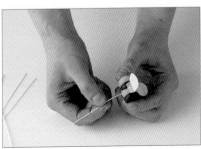

6 Use the reserved black marzipan and the sugarpaste icing to make the faces. Then cut the florist's wire into various lengths and pierce the bees from underneath. Once secure, press the other end of the wire into the cake. The wire must be removed before serving.

Mobile Phone Cake

For the upwardly mobile, this novel cake just has to be the business!

Serves 8–10

INGREDIENTS

1 x quantity quick-mix sponge cake, baked
   in a 23 x 13 cm/9 x 5 in loaf tin (pan)
30 ml/2 tbsp apricot glaze
1 x quantity sugarpaste (fondant) icing
black food colouring
10 small square sweets
30–45 ml/2–3 tbsp icing
   (confectioners') sugar
2.5–5 ml/½–1 tsp water

1 Turn the cake upside down. Make
a 2.5 cm/1 in diagonal cut 2.5 cm/
1 in from one end. Cut down
vertically to remove the wedge.
Remove the middle of the cake to the
wedge depth up to 4 cm/1½ in from
the other end.

2 Place the cake on a board and
brush with apricot glaze. Tint 275 g/
10 oz/1¾ cups of the sugarpaste icing
black. Use to cover the cake,
smoothing it over the carved shape.
Reserve the trimmings.

3 Tint the remaining sugarpaste icing
grey. Cut a piece to fit the hollowed
centre, leaving a 1 cm/½ in border, and
another piece 2.5 cm/1 in square.
Stamp out the centre of the square
with a diamond-shape cutter. Secure
all the pieces on the cake with water.

4 Position the sweets and a small
piece of foil for the display panel. For
the glacé icing, mix the icing sugar
with the water and tint black. With a
small round nozzle, pipe border lines
around the edges of the phone,
including the grey pieces of sugarpaste.
Pipe the numbers on the keys.

5 Roll a sausage shape from the
reserved black sugarpaste for the aerial.
Indent one side of the top with a knife
and secure the aerial with water.

VARIATION: If preferred, use a
little extra sugarpaste for the dial
pad instead of the sweets.

Artist's Box & Palette

Making cakes is an art in itself, and this cake proves it. It is the perfect celebration cake for artists of all ages.

Serves 30

INGREDIENTS
1¼ x quantity rich fruit cake, baked in a
   20 cm/8 in square tin (pan)
45 ml/3 tbsp apricot glaze
1 x quantity marzipan
2⅓ x quantity sugarpaste (fondant) icing
chestnut, yellow, blue, black, silver,
   paprika, green and mulberry
   food colouring
90 g/3½ oz/⅔ cup royal icing

1 Brush the cake with the apricot glaze. Cover in marzipan and leave to dry overnight.

2 Make a template of a painter's palette that will fit the cake top. Tint 175 g/6 oz/generous 1 cup of the sugarpaste very pale chestnut. Cut out the palette shape from the tinted sugarpaste, place on baking parchment and leave to dry overnight.

3 Tint 450 g/1 lb/3 cups of the sugarpaste icing dark chestnut. Use to cover the cake. Secure the cake on a board with royal icing. Leave to dry.

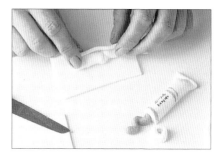

4 Divide half the remaining sugarpaste icing into seven equal parts and tint yellow, blue, black, silver, paprika, green and mulberry. Make all the decorative pieces for the box and palette, using the remaining white sugarpaste for the paint tubes. Leave to dry on baking parchment.

5 Paint black markings on the paint tubes and chestnut wood markings on the box.

6 Position all the sugarpaste pieces on the cake and board using royal icing. Leave to dry.

COOK'S TIP: Start modelling the cake decorations the day before assembling.

Glittering Star Cake

With a quick flick of a paintbrush you can give a sparkling effect to this glittering cake.

Serves 20–25

INGREDIENTS
1 x quantity rich fruit cake, baked in a
   20 cm/8 in round tin (pan)
40 ml/2½ tbsp apricot glaze
1½ x quantity marzipan
450 g/1 lb/3 cups sugarpaste (fondant) icing
silver, gold, lilac shimmer, red sparkle, glitter
   green and primrose sparkle food colouring
   and powder tints
90 g/3½ oz/⅔ cup royal icing

1 Brush the cake with the apricot glaze. Use two-thirds of the marzipan to cover the cake. Leave to dry overnight.

2 Cover the cake with the sugarpaste icing. Leave to dry.

3 Place the cake on a large sheet of baking parchment. Dilute a little powdered silver food colouring and, using a loaded paintbrush, flick it all over the cake to give a spattered effect. Allow to dry.

4 Make templates of two different-size moon shapes and three irregular star shapes. Divide the remaining marzipan into six pieces and tint silver, gold, lilac shimmer, red sparkle, glitter green and primrose. Using the templates, cut into stars and moons, cutting some of the stars in half.

5 Place the cut-outs on baking parchment, brush each with its own colour powder tint. Allow to dry.

6 Secure the cake on a board with royal icing. Arrange the stars and moons at different angles all over the cake, attaching with royal icing, and position the halved stars upright as though coming out of the cake. Allow to set.

COOK'S TIP: Stored in an airtight container, the cake will keep for up to 3 weeks.

Lucky Horseshoe Cake

This horseshoe-shaped cake, made to wish "good luck", is made from a round cake cut to shape. Use a crimping tool for the edge.

Serves 30–35

INGREDIENTS
1½ x quantity rich fruit cake, baked in a
    25 cm/10 in round tin (pan)
60 ml/4 tbsp apricot glaze
2 x quantity marzipan
3 x quantity sugarpaste (fondant) icing
peach and blue food colouring
3 mm/⅛ in wide blue ribbon
edible silver balls
90 g/3½ oz/⅔ cup royal icing

1 Make a horseshoe template and use to shape the cake. Brush the cake with apricot glaze. Cover the cake with marzipan using the template and 350 g/12 oz/2¼ cups of marzipan for the top, and measuring the inside and outside of the cake to cover with the remaining marzipan. Place on a board and leave overnight.

2 Tint 800 g/1¾ lb/5¼ cups of the sugarpaste icing peach. Cover the cake in the same way. Crimp the top edge.

3 Draw and measure the ribbon insertion on the template. Cut 13 pieces of ribbon fractionally longer than each slit. Make the slits in the icing through the template with a scalpel. Insert the ribbon with a pointed tool. Leave to dry overnight.

4 Tint half the remaining sugarpaste icing pale blue. Cut out nine blue small horseshoe shapes. Mark each horseshoe with a sharp knife. Cut out 12 large and 15 small blossoms with blossom cutters. Press a silver ball into the centres of the larger blossoms. Dry. Repeat with the white icing. Decorate the cake, securing with royal icing.

Bluebird Bon Voyage Cake

This cake with its marble-effect sky is sure to see someone off on an exciting journey in a very special way.

Serves 12–15

INGREDIENTS
1 x quantity royal icing
blue food colouring
2½ x quantity sugarpaste (fondant) icing
1 x quantity Madeira cake, baked in a
    20 cm/8 in round tin (pan)
1 x quantity butter icing
45 ml/3 tbsp apricot glaze
edible silver balls
thin pale blue ribbon

1 Make two-thirds of the royal icing softer, to use for filling in. Make the rest stiffer for the outlines and further piping. Tint the softer icing bright blue. Cover and leave overnight.

2 Make two different-size bird templates, and use to draw four large and five small birds on to baking parchment. Turn the paper over. Using a No 1. writing nozzle and white icing, pipe the outlines, then fill in with blue icing. Leave to dry for at least 2 days.

3 Tint two-thirds of the sugarpaste icing blue. Form all the icing into small rolls and place them alternately together on a work surface. Form into a round and lightly knead to marble.

4 Cut the cake horizontally into three and sandwich together with the butter icing. Brush with apricot glaze. Roll out the marbled icing and use to cover the cake and a board. Place the cake on the board, flush with the edge.

5 Using the No. 1 writing nozzle and the stiffer royal icing, pipe a wavy line around the edge of the board. Position the balls evenly in the icing. Secure the birds to the cake with royal icing. Pipe beads of white icing for eyes and stick on a ball. Drape the ribbon between the beaks, securing with icing.

COOK'S TIP: The finished cake can be kept for up to 1 week in an airtight container.

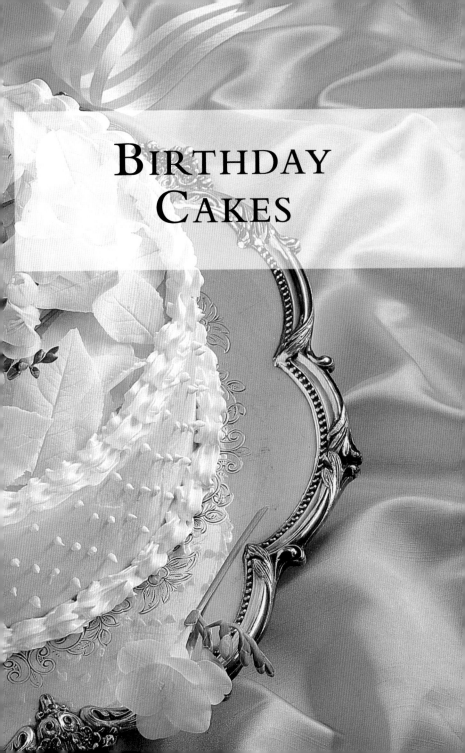

BIRTHDAY
CAKES

Flickering Candle Cake

Stripy icing candles are flickering and ready to blow out on this birthday celebration cake for all ages.

Serves 15–20

INGREDIENTS
1⅓ x quantity Madeira cake mix
1 x quantity butter icing
45 ml/3 tbsp apricot glaze
2½ x quantity sugarpaste (fondant) icing
pink, yellow, purple and jade
    food colouring
edible silver balls
edible-ink pens

1 Preheat the oven to 160°C/325°F/
Gas 3. Grease and line a 20 cm/8 in
square cake tin (pan). Spoon in the
mixture, tap the tin lightly to level and
bake for 1¼–1½ hours, until a metal
skewer inserted into the centre comes
out clean. Place the tin on a wire rack
for 10 minutes, then turn the cake out
on to the rack to cool.

2 Cut the cake horizontally into
three layers. Sandwich the layers
together with the butter icing and
brush the cake with the apricot glaze.

3 Roll out 500 g/1¼ lb/3¾ cups of
the sugarpaste icing on a surface lightly
dusted with icing (confectioners')
sugar. Use the sugarpaste icing to
cover the cake completely and trim
the edges neatly. Place the cake on a
23 cm/9 in square cake board.

4 Divide the remaining icing into
quarters and colour them pink, yellow,
purple and jade. Roll out the jade
icing and cut into six 1 cm/½ in strips
of unequal length, but each long
enough to go up the side and on to
the top of the cake. Make a diagonal
cut at one end of each. Roll out the
yellow icing and stamp out six flames
with a leaf-shaped cutter. Place a silver
ball in each flame.

5 Stick the candles on the cake with
a little water. Mould small strips,
fractionally longer than the candles'
width, from the yellow and purple
icing. Stick alternate colour strips on
the candles at a slight angle. Stick the
flames at the top.

6 Roll out the pink icing and the
remaining purple icing and cut out
wavy pieces. Stick on the cake above
the candles. Gather the pink trimmings
into a ball.

7 Roll out the remaining yellow icing and stamp out circles with a small round cutter or the end of a piping nozzle. Make small balls from the remaining pink icing and stick them to the yellow circles. Press a silver ball into the centre of each decoration. Stick the decorations around the bottom of the cake.

8 Draw wavy lines and dots coming from the purple and pink wavy icing with food colouring pens. Decorate the sides of the cake board with jade ribbon, securing it with a little softened sugar paste.

Birthday Parcel

Here is a birthday cake that is all wrapped up and ready to eat. Change the pattern by using different shaped cutters.

Serves 10

INGREDIENTS
⅔ x quantity Madeira cake mix
¾ x quantity orange-flavour butter icing
45 ml/3 tbsp apricot jam, warmed
    and sieved
1⅓ x quantity sugarpaste (fondant) icing
blue, orange and green food colouring

1 Preheat the oven to 160°C/325°F/ Gas 3. Grease and line a 15 cm/6 in square cake tin (pan). Spoon in the mixture, tap to level it and bake for 1 hour 10 minutes, or until a metal skewer inserted into the centre comes out clean. Place the tin on a wire rack for 10 minutes, then turn the cake out on to the rack to cool completely.

2 Cut the cake in half horizontally and sandwich together with the butter icing. Brush the cake with the jam. Colour three-quarters of the sugarpaste icing blue. Divide the remaining icing in half and colour one half orange and the other green.

3 Roll out the blue icing on a surface lightly dusted with icing (confectioners') sugar and use it to cover the cake. Place on the cake board. Stamp out circles and triangles from the icing with cocktail cutters, lifting out to expose the cake.

4 Roll out the orange and green icing and stamp out circles and triangles. Fill the holes in the blue icing with the orange and green shapes. Gather the trimmings to use for the ribbons.

5 Roll out the orange trimmings and cut three strips about 2 cm/¾ in wide and long enough to go over each corner of the cake. Roll out the green trimmings and cut three very thin strips the same length as the orange ones. Place the orange and green strips next to each other to give three striped ribbons and stick together with a little water.

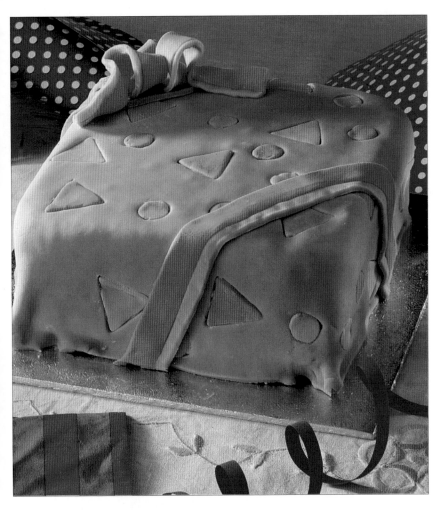

6 Stick one striped ribbon over one corner of the cake. Stick a second strip over the opposite corner. Cut the remaining ribbon in half. Bend each half to make loops and stick both to the ribbon over one corner of the cake to form a loose bow.

Eighteenth Birthday Cake

A really striking and sophisticated cake for a lucky someone celebrating their eighteenth birthday.

Serves 80

INGREDIENTS
1⅓ x quantity rich fruit cake mix
45 ml/3 tbsp apricot glaze
2½ x quantity marzipan
4⅔ x quantity sugarpaste (fondant) icing
black food colouring
30 ml/2 tbsp royal icing

1 Preheat the oven to 150°C/300°F/Gas 2. Grease and line a 33.5 x 20 cm/13½ x 8 in diamond-shaped deep cake tin (pan). Spoon in the mixture, smooth the top, make a slight dip in the centre and bake for 3¼–3¾ hours, until a metal skewer put into the centre comes out clean. Cool in the tin, then turn out.

2 Brush the cake with glaze and place it on a cake board. Roll out the marzipan on a surface lightly dusted with icing (confectioners') sugar. Use to cover the cake and trim the edges.

3 Roll out 1.1 kg/2½ lb/3⅓ cups of the sugarpaste icing on a surface lightly dusted with icing sugar and use to cover the cake, trimming the edges. Knead the trimmings into the remaining sugarpaste and colour it black. Roll out two-thirds and cut into four strips the width and length of each section of the cake board.

4 Brush the board with glaze, place each strip in position and trim. Roll out one-quarter of the remaining sugarpaste and stamp out the number 18 with a special cutter or using a template. Leave on a piece of foam sponge to dry. Roll out some more sugarpaste and use a cocktail cutter to stamp out 40 triangles for the bow ties and 20 for the glasses.

5 Roll out some more sugarpaste and stamp out 20 circles for the music notes and 10 bases for the glasses with a tiny round cutter. Cut the bases in half. Cut out thin strips for the tails of the notes and the stems of the glasses.

6 Colour the royal icing black and spoon into a piping (icing) bag fitted with a No. 1 plain writing nozzle. With tiny beads of icing, join the bow ties together, attach the music notes to their tails and the glasses to their stems and bases. Leave to dry.

7 Arrange the numbers, notes, glasses and bow ties over the top of the cake, then stick them down with a bead of icing. Finish the decoration with black and white ribbons.

Twenty-first Birthday Cake

This cake looks good in any pale colour or simply white. Add the colour with the ribbons and write your own message.

Serves 80

INGREDIENTS

1⅔ x quantity rich fruit
   cake mix
45 ml/3 tbsp apricot glaze
2½ x quantity marzipan
2 x quantity royal icing
blue food colouring
500 g/1¼ lb ready-made
   petal paste
cornflour (cornstarch), for dusting

1 Preheat the oven to 150°C/300°F/ Gas 2. Grease and line a 25 cm/10 in round deep cake tin (pan). Spoon in the mixture, smooth the top, make a depression in the centre and bake for 3¾ hours, until a metal skewer inserted into the centre comes out clean. Cool in the tin, then turn out.

2 Brush the cake with glaze and place on a 30 cm/12 in round cake board. Roll out the marzipan on a surface dusted with icing (confectioners') sugar. Use to cover the cake and trim the edges.

3 Colour the royal icing pale blue. Flat-ice the top and side of the cake with three layers of smooth royal icing, leaving each to dry before adding the next, then ice the cake board.

4 Colour the petal paste pale blue. Roll out one-third on a surface lightly dusted with cornflour. Stamp out two squares with a 7.5 cm/3 in fluted cutter. Stamp out an oval from one square with a 5 cm/2 in plain cutter. Make two tiny holes with a No. 2 plain writing nozzle on the left hand edge on both squares to match. Continue to make a cut-out pattern all around the front of the card. Leave on a piece of foam sponge to dry.

5 Roll out some more petal paste. Stamp out 25 shapes with a club-shaped cocktail cutter, allowing for breakage. Use a tiny petal cutter to cut out three shapes on each piece. Leave to dry thoroughly. Roll out the remaining paste and stamp out two end shapes for the keys with the club cutter. Cut out the remaining parts of the key shapes with a sharp knife. Pattern the keys with tiny cutters. Leave to dry.

6 Tie plain pale and royal blue ribbons around the board, securing with a pin. Fit looped royal blue ribbon around the side of the cake and secure with a bead of icing.

7 Spoon blue icing into a piping bag fitted with a No. 3 plain writing nozzle. Arrange 18 cut-out sugar pieces around the top edge of the cake and secure with a bead of icing. Leave to dry. Pipe a shell edging around the base and between the cut-outs on top.

8 Write your message on the plain card with a food colouring pen and decorate the keys. Thread narrow royal blue ribbon around the card and through the matching holes to join it. Tie in a bow with long ends.

9 Thread matching ribbon through the cut-out sugar pieces, joining the ends with a bead of icing. Tie a bow and stick it to the side of the cake with a bead of icing. Attach the card and the keys with icing and leave to dry.

Flower Birthday Cake

Pretty piped sugar flowers and coral and white ribbons decorate this charming birthday cake.

Serves 40

INGREDIENTS
¾ x quantity rich fruit cake mix
30 ml/2 tbsp apricot glaze
1½ x quantity marzipan
3¾ x quantity royal icing
yellow and orange food colouring

1 Preheat the oven to 150°C/300°F/Gas 2. Grease and line a 18 cm/7 in round deep cake tin (pan). Spoon in the mixture, smooth the top, make a slight depression in the centre and bake for 2½–2¾ hours, until a metal skewer inserted into the centre comes out clean. Leave to cool in the tin, then turn out.

2 Brush the cake with the apricot glaze. Roll out the marzipan on a surface lightly dusted with icing (confectioners') sugar and use to cover the cake. Transfer to a 23 cm/9 in round cake board. Flat-ice the top and side of the cake with three layers of royal icing, leaving each to dry, then ice the cake board.

3 Snip an inverted V shape off the point of a baking parchment piping bag. Fit another bag with a petal nozzle, a third with a No. 1 plain writing nozzle and a fourth with a medium star nozzle.

4 Colour one-third of the remaining icing yellow and then colour 15 ml/1 tbsp of the icing orange. Pipe the narcissi using the petal nozzle for the petals and the writing nozzle for the centres. Make four white narcissi with yellow centres and nine yellow narcissi with orange centres.

5 Pipe nine simple white flowers with the snipped bag and add yellow centres with the plain nozzle. Leave to dry on baking parchment.

6 Arrange the flowers on the top of the cake, securing them with a little icing. With white icing and a star nozzle, pipe shell edging all around the top and base of the cake.

7 With white icing and a No. 2 plain writing nozzle, pipe "Happy Birthday" on either side of the flowers.

8 Place white ribbon around the board and secure with a pin. Place coral ribbon around the board and side of the cake, securing with a bead of icing. Over-pipe the writing with orange icing and a No. 1 plain writing nozzle. Tie a bow and stick to the cake with a bead of icing. Leave to dry.

Birthday Bowl of Strawberries

With its hand-painted picture and moulded fruit, this is the ideal cake to celebrate a summer birthday.

Serves 20

INGREDIENTS
1 x quantity Madeira cake mix
1 x quantity butter icing
45 ml/3 tbsp apricot glaze
2 x quantity sugarpaste (fondant) icing
pink, red, yellow, green and claret
    food colouring
cornflour (cornstarch), for dusting
yellow powdered food colouring

1 Preheat the oven to 160°C/325°F/Gas 3. Grease and line a 20 cm/8 in petal-shaped cake tin (pan). Spoon in the mixture, tap lightly to level and bake for 1¼ hours, until a metal skewer inserted into the centre comes out clean. Place the tin on a wire rack for 10 minutes, then turn the cake out on to the rack to cool.

2 Colour the butter icing pink. Cut the cake horizontally into three and sandwich together with the butter icing. Brush with the glaze. Roll out 500g/1¼ lb/3¾ cups of the sugarpaste icing on a surface that has been lightly dusted with icing (confectioners') sugar. Use to cover the cake and trim. Place the cake on a 25 cm/10 in petal-shaped cake board and leave to dry for 12 hours.

3 Colour three-quarters of the remaining sugarpaste red. Divide the rest in half and colour one half yellow and the other green. Dust your hands with cornflour and mould the red icing into strawberries.

4 Make tiny oval shapes from the yellow icing and press on to the strawberries. Shape the green icing into flat circles and snip round the edges with scissors. Curl the edges slightly and stick to the top of the strawberries with a little water. Leave to dry on baking parchment.

5 Put red, green, yellow and claret food colouring on a palette and dilute slightly with a little water. Paint the outline of the bowl with the claret food colouring, then fill in the pattern. Add highlights with a little of the yellow powdered food colouring.

6 Finish painting the pattern, filling in the strawberries in the bowl and around the edge of the cake.

7 Decorate the cake with red and green ribbons. Stick two moulded strawberries to the top and arrange the others around the bottom.

Frosted Flower Cake

If pansies are not in season, use other edible flowers – just coordinate the colour of the icing and decoration.

Serves 20–25

INGREDIENTS
1 x quantity rich fruit cake mix
45 ml/3 tbsp apricot glaze
1½ x quantity marzipan
1⅔ x quantity royal icing
orange food colouring
about 7 orange and
    purple pansies
1 egg white, lightly beaten
caster (superfine) sugar, for frosting

1 Preheat the oven to 150°C/300°F/ Gas 2. Grease and line a 20 cm/8 in round deep cake tin (pan). Spoon in the mixture, smooth the top, make a slight depression in the centre and bake for 2¾–3¼ hours, until a metal skewer inserted into the centre comes out clean. Cool in the tin, then turn out on to a wire rack.

2 Brush the cake with the glaze. Roll out the marzipan on a surface lightly dusted with icing (confectioners') sugar and use to cover the cake.

3 Secure the cake to a 25 cm/10 in round cake board with a little icing. Colour one-quarter of the icing pale orange. Flat-ice the cake with three or four layers of icing, using orange for the top and white for the sides. Leave each layer to dry.

4 Wash the pansies and dry on kitchen paper. Leave a short piece of stem attached. Brush both sides of the petals with egg white. Holding the flowers by the stems, sprinkle them evenly with sugar, then shake off the excess. Leave to dry on a wire rack covered with baking parchment.

5 Spoon some white icing into a piping (icing) bag fitted with a No. 19 star nozzle. Pipe a row of scrolls around the top of the cake. Pipe a second row of scrolls in the opposite direction, directly underneath. Pipe another row of scrolls around the bottom of the cake.

6 Spoon some orange icing into a piping bag fitted with a No. 1 writing nozzle. Pipe around the outline of the top of each scroll. Pipe a row of orange dots under the reverse scrolls and a double row of dots above the bottom row of scrolls. Arrange the pansies on top of the cake. Decorate with a wide and a narrow purple ribbon.

Cloth of Roses Cake

It is almost too pretty to eat, so make this for a very special birthday.

Serves 20–25

INGREDIENTS
1 x quantity rich fruit cake mix
45 ml/3 tbsp apricot glaze
1½ x quantity marzipan
2⅔ x quantity sugarpaste (fondant) icing
yellow, orange and green food colouring
cornflour (cornstarch), for dusting
⅛ x quantity royal icing

1 Preheat the oven to 150°C/300°F/ Gas 2. Grease and line a 20 cm/8 in round deep cake tin (pan). Spoon in the mixture, smooth the top, make a slight depression in the centre and bake for 2¾–3¼ hours, until a metal skewer inserted into the centre comes out clean. Cool in the tin, then turn out on to a wire rack.

2 Brush the cake with the glaze. Roll out the marzipan on a surface lightly dusted with icing (confectioners') sugar and use to cover the cake. Cut a template from baking parchment: draw a 25 cm/10 in circle. Use a 7 cm/ 2¾ in plain cutter as a guide to draw half circles 2.5 cm/1 in wide around the outside of the large circle. Cut out.

3 Colour 350 g/12 oz/2¼ cups of the sugarpaste pale yellow and roll out on a work surface lightly dusted with icing sugar. Use to cover the cake. Place the cake on a 25 cm/10 in cake board.

4 Colour 350 g/12 oz/2¼ cups of the remaining sugarpaste pale orange and roll out to a 30 cm/12 in circle. Place the template on the icing and cut out. Brush the cake with water and cover with the orange icing so that the scallops fall just over the edge. Curl them slightly and leave to dry.

5 Reserve about one-quarter of the remaining sugarpaste for the leaves and divide the rest into quarters. Colour them pale yellow, deep yellow, orange and marbled yellow and orange.

6 Dust your hands with cornflour. To make the roses, take a small ball of sugarpaste and form into a cone. Form a piece into a petal slightly thicker at the base. Press around the cone, so it sits above the top. Curl the end.

7 Repeat with several more petals, making them slightly larger each time and attaching them so they just overlap. Cut off the base. Make about 18 roses and dry on baking parchment.

8 Colour the remaining sugarpaste green. Roll out thinly and stamp out about 24 leaves with a petal cutter. Leave to dry on baking parchment.

9 Arrange the leaves and roses on the cake, securing them with a bead of royal icing. Decorate the cake with a thin yellow ribbon.

243

Celebration Rose and Fruit Cake

Covered with delicately flavoured rose water icing, this luscious cake is decorated with frosted roses.

Serves 20–25

INGREDIENTS
1 x quantity rich fruit cake mix
900 g/2 lb/5½ cups icing
   (confectioners') sugar
3 egg whites
5 ml/1 tsp distilled rose water
2.5 ml/½ tsp lemon juice
120 ml/4 fl oz/½ cup liquid glucose
45 ml/3 tbsp rose jelly
8–9 roses
caster (superfine) sugar, for frosting

1 Preheat the oven to 150°C/300°F/ Gas 2. Grease and line a 20 cm/8 in round deep cake tin (pan). Spoon in the mixture, smooth the top, make a slight depression in the centre and bake for 2¾–3¼ hours, until a metal skewer inserted into the centre comes out clean. Cool in the tin, then turn out on to a wire rack.

2 Sift the icing sugar into a bowl and beat in two of the egg whites, the rose water, lemon juice and liquid glucose with a wooden spoon. Knead until the mixture forms a smooth, pliable icing.

3 Transfer the cake to a 25 cm/10 in round cake board. Brush the top and side with the rose jelly, warming it first, if necessary. Roll out the icing on a surface lightly dusted with icing sugar. Position the icing on the cake, smoothing the top and the sides. Frill out at the base of the cake and trim off any excess.

4 Wash the roses and dry on kitchen paper. Leave a little of the stem still attached. Lightly beat the remaining egg white. Brush both sides of the rose petals with the egg white. Holding the flowers by the stems, sprinkle them evenly with sugar, then shake off the excess. Leave to dry on a wire rack covered with baking parchment.

5 If necessary, trim the stems of the roses. Arrange three roses on top of the cake and the remainder around the frill at the base.

Jazzy Chocolate Gâteau

With its modern and sophisticated appearance, this would make a good birthday cake for a teenager.

Serves 12–15

INGREDIENTS
2 x quantity chocolate-flavoured quick-mix
   sponge mix
75 g/3 oz plain (semisweet) chocolate
75 g/3 oz white chocolate
½ x quantity fudge frosting
120 ml/8 tbsp chocolate
   hazelnut spread

FOR THE COFFEE GLACE ICING
115 g/4 oz/1 cup icing (confectioners') sugar
5 ml/1 tsp weak coffee
30 ml/2 tbsp warm water

1 Preheat the oven to 160°C/325°F/ Gas 3. Grease and line two 20 cm/8 in round cake tins (pans). Divide the cake mixture equally between the tins, smooth the surfaces and bake for 20–30 minutes, until a metal skewer inserted into the centres comes out clean. Turn out on to a wire rack.

2 Meanwhile, cover a large baking sheet with baking parchment. Melt the plain and white chocolate in separate bowls over pans of simmering water, stirring until smooth, then pour on to the baking sheet.

3 Spread out evenly with a palette knife or metal spatula and leave to cool until firm enough to cut. When the chocolate no longer feels sticky, cut out random shapes and set aside.

4 Sandwich the two cooled cakes together with the fudge frosting and transfer to a serving plate.

5 To make the icing, sift the sugar into a bowl, stir in the coffee and gradually stir in sufficient water to give the consistency of thick cream. Beat until smooth. Spread the icing on top of the cake almost to the edges.

6 Spread the side of the cake with enough chocolate hazelnut spread to cover. Arrange the chocolate pieces around the side of the cake, pressing them into the spread. Spoon about 45 ml/3 tbsp of the spread into a piping bag fitted with a No. 1 plain nozzle and pipe "jazzy" lines over the icing.

Divine Chocolate Cake

This very rich cake would be the best possible way to say "Happy Birthday" to a chocoholic.

Serves 18–20

INGREDIENTS
225 g/8 oz fine quality dark (bittersweet)
  chocolate, chopped
115 g/4 oz/½ cup unsalted (sweet) butter,
  cut into pieces
170 ml/5½ fl oz/⅔ cup water
250 g/9 oz/1¼ cups granulated sugar
10 ml/2 tsp vanilla essence (extract)
2 eggs, separated
170 ml/5½ fl oz/⅔ cup buttermilk or
  sour cream
365 g/12½ oz/2 cups plain (all-purpose) flour
10 ml/2 tsp baking powder
5 ml/1 tsp bicarbonate of soda
  (baking soda)
pinch of cream of tartar
chocolate curls, raspberries and icing
  (confectioners') sugar, to decorate

FOR THE CHOCOLATE FUDGE FILLING
450 g/1 lb fine quality couverture
  chocolate or dark (bittersweet)
  chocolate, chopped
225 g/8 oz/1 cup unsalted (sweet) butter
75 ml/3 fl oz/⅓ cup brandy or rum
215 g/7½ oz/¾ cup seedless
  raspberry preserve

FOR THE CHOCOLATE GANACHE GLAZE
250 ml/8 fl oz/1 cup double (heavy) cream
225 g/8 oz couverture chocolate or dark
  (bittersweet) chocolate, chopped
30 ml/2 tbsp brandy or rum

1 Preheat the oven to 180°C/350°F/ Gas 4. Grease and line a 25 cm/10 in springform tin (pan).

2 Heat the chocolate, butter and water in a small pan, stirring frequently, until smooth. Remove from the heat, transfer to a bowl, beat in the sugar and cool. Lightly beat the egg yolks, then beat into the chocolate mixture with the vanilla essence.

3 Fold in the buttermilk or sour cream. Sift the flour, baking powder and bicarbonate of soda into a bowl, then fold into the chocolate mixture. Beat the egg whites and cream of tartar with an electric mixer until stiff peaks form, then fold into the chocolate mixture.

4 Pour the mixture into the tin and bake for 45–50 minutes, until the cake begins to shrink from the side of the tin. Place the tin on a wire rack for 10 minutes, then turn the cake out on to the rack to cool.

5 To make the filling, heat the chocolate, butter and 60 ml/4 tbsp of the brandy or rum in a pan, stirring frequently, until smooth. Remove from the heat and ser aside to cool and thicken.

6 Cut the cake horizontally into three layers. Heat the raspberry preserve and remaining brandy or rum, stirring frequently until smooth. Spread thinly over each layer and leave to set.

7 Place the bottom layer in the cleaned tin. Spread with half the filling, top with the second layer and spread with the remaining filling. Top with the final layer, coated side down.

8 Gently press together, cover and chill for 4–6 hours or overnight. Remove the cake from the tin and set on a wire rack over a tray.

9 To make the glaze, bring the cream to the boil in a pan. Remove from the heat, add all the chocolate and stir until smooth. Stir in the brandy or rum, strain and set aside for 4–5 minutes to thicken. Whisk until smooth and shiny.

10 Pour the glaze over the cake, smoothing with a metal spatula. Leave to set, then transfer to a serving plate and decorate with chocolate curls and raspberries. Dust with icing sugar.

Chocolate Box with Caramel Mousse & Berries

For chocolate lovers this luscious chocolate box makes the ideal birthday cake. Choose berries and fruit that are in season

Serves 8–10

INGREDIENTS
275 g/10 oz plain (semisweet) chocolate, broken into pieces

FOR THE CARAMEL MOUSSE
4 x 50 g/2 oz chocolate-coated caramel bars, coarsely chopped
20 ml/4 tsp milk or water
350 ml/12 fl oz/1½ cups double (heavy) cream
1 egg white

FOR THE CARAMEL SHARDS
120 ml/8 tbsp granulated sugar
50 ml/2 fl oz/¼ cup water

FOR THE TOPPING
115 g/4 oz white chocolate, chopped
350 ml/12 fl oz/1½ cups double (heavy) cream
450 g/1 lb mixed berries or cut-up fruits, such as raspberries, strawberries and blackberries or nectarine and orange segments

1 To make the box, line a 23 cm/9 in baking tin (pan) with foil. Melt the plain chocolate in a bowl over a pan of simmering water, stirring constantly until smooth. Pour into the tin and keep tilting to coat the base and sides evenly. Chill for 45 minutes, until firm.

2 To make the mousse, put the caramel bars and milk or water in a bowl set over a pan of simmering water and stir until melted. Remove from the heat and cool for 10 minutes, stirring occasionally. Whip the cream with an electric mixer until soft peaks form. Stir a spoonful of the cream into the caramel mixture, then fold in the rest. In a separate bowl, beat the egg white until just stiff, then fold it into the mousse. Pour into the chocolate box and chill for 6–8 hours or overnight.

3 To make the caramel shards, lightly oil a baking sheet. Dissolve the sugar in the water over low heat, stirring gently, then boil for 4–5 minutes, until the mixture turns pale gold. Immediately pour on to the oiled sheet, tilting to spread evenly. Do not touch the hot caramel. Cool, then lift off the sheet and break into pieces with a metal spatula. Set aside.

4 For the topping, heat the white chocolate with 120 ml/4 fl oz/½ cup cream over a low heat, stirring frequently, until smooth. Strain and leave to cool, stirring occasionally. Beat the remaining cream with an electric mixer until firm peaks form. Stir a spoonful of cream into the chocolate mixture, then fold in the remainder.

5 Remove the mousse-filled box from the foil by peeling it carefully from the sides and the base. Slide on to a serving plate. Spoon the chocolate-cream mixture into a piping bag fitted with a medium star nozzle and pipe rosettes or shells over the surface of the mousse. Decorate with fruits and caramel shards.

White Chocolate Cake

Make this superb cake for an extra special birthday, such as a fiftieth.

Serves 40–50

INGREDIENTS

FOR THE TWO CAKES
2 x 600 g/1 lb 5 oz/4 cups plain
    (all-purpose) flour
2 x 10 ml/2 tsp bicarbonate of soda
    (baking soda)
2 x pinch of salt
2 x 225 g/8 oz white chocolate, chopped
2 x 250 ml/8 fl oz/1 cup whipping cream
2 x 225 g/8 oz/1 cup unsalted (sweet) butter
2 x 400 g/14 oz/2 cups caster (superfine) sugar
2 x 6 eggs
2 x 10 ml/2 tsp lemon essence (extract)
2 x grated rind of 1 lemon
2 x 325 ml/11 fl oz/1⅓ cups buttermilk
whipped cream, chocolate leaves and fresh
    flowers, to decorate

FOR THE LEMON SYRUP
90 g/3½ oz/½ cup granulated sugar
120 ml/4 fl oz/½ cup water
30 ml/2 tbsp fresh lemon juice

FOR THE BUTTERCREAM (2 BATCHES)
2 x 350 g/12 oz white chocolate, chopped
2 x 500 g/1¼ lb/2½ cups cream cheese
2 x 275 g/10 oz unsalted (sweet) butter
2 x 30 ml/2 tbsp fresh lemon juice
2 x 2.5 ml/½ tsp lemon essence (extract)

FOR ASSEMBLING
175 g/6 oz/⅔ cup lemon curd
50–115 g/2–4 oz/4–8 tbsp unsalted (sweet)
    butter, softened

1 Start by making one cake. Preheat the oven to 180°C/350°F/Gas 4. Grease and line a 30 cm/12 in cake tin (pan).

2 Sift the flour, bicarbonate of soda and salt into a bowl. Heat the chocolate and cream over a medium heat, stirring, until smooth. Set aside to cool. Beat the butter with an electric mixer until creamy, add the sugar and beat for 2–3 minutes. Beat in the eggs. Slowly beat in the chocolate mixture, lemon essence and rind. On low speed, alternately beat in the flour in four batches and the buttermilk in three batches until smooth.

3 Pour into the tin and bake for 1 hour, until a metal skewer inserted into the centre comes out clean. Place the tin on a wire rack for 10 minutes, then turn out on to the rack to cool. Make a second cake. For the syrup, dissolve the sugar in the water over a medium heat, stirring. Off the heat, stir in the lemon juice and let cool.

4 To make the buttercream, put the chocolate in a bowl set over a pan of simmering water and stir until melted. Remove from the heat and cool slightly. Beat the cream cheese until smooth with an electric mixer. Gradually beat in the chocolate, then the butter, lemon juice and essence. Make a second batch.

5 To assemble, cut each cake in half horizontally. Spoon the syrup over each layer, allowing it to soak in, then repeat. Sandwich the layers of each cake together with lemon curd.

6 Gently beat the buttercream, then spread one-quarter on top of one cake. Place the other cake on top. Spread a little softened butter over the top and side. Chill for 15 minutes. Place the cake on a serving plate and spread the remaining buttercream on the top and side.

7 Spoon the whipped cream into a piping bag fitted with a small star nozzle and pipe shells carefully around the edges. Decorate with the leaves and flowers.

Chocolate Fruit Birthday Cake

A moist Madeira chocolate cake is decorated with eye-catching fruit moulded from coloured marzipan.

Serves 30

INGREDIENTS
1 x quantity chocolate-flavoured
   Madeira cake mix (see Cook's Tip)
45 ml/3 tbsp apricot glaze
1 x quantity marzipan
1⅓ x quantity chocolate fudge frosting
red, yellow, orange, green and purple
   food colouring
cloves
angelica strips

1 Preheat the oven to 160°C/325°F/ Gas 3. Grease and line an 18 cm/7 in square cake tin (pan). Spoon in the mixture, tap lightly to level the surface and bake for 1¼ hours, until a metal skewer inserted into the centre comes out clean. Place the tin on a wire rack for 10 minutes, then turn the cake out on to the rack to cool.

2 Cut a slice off the top of the cake to level, if necessary, then invert on to a 20 cm/8 in square cake board. Brush with the glaze. Roll out two-thirds of the marzipan on a surface lightly dusted with icing (confectioners') sugar to a 25 cm/10 in square. Use to cover and trim the cake. Reserve the trimmings.

3 Place the cake on a wire rack over a tray and pour over the warm fudge frosting, spreading quickly with a metal spatula. Leave for 10 minutes, then return to the cake board.

4 Spoon the frosting from the tray into a piping (icing) bag fitted with a medium gâteau nozzle. Pipe a row of stars around the top edge and base of the cake. Leave to set.

5 Using the reserved marzipan, food colouring, cloves and angelica strips, model a selection of fruits.

6 Fit a strip of looped yellow ribbon around the cake and secure with a pin. Decorate the top of the cake with the colourful marzipan fruits.

COOK'S TIP: To flavour the cake mix, omit the lemon rind and vanilla essence (extract) and stir in 15 ml/1 tbsp unsweetened cocoa powder blended with 15 ml/1 tbsp boiling water just before adding the eggs.

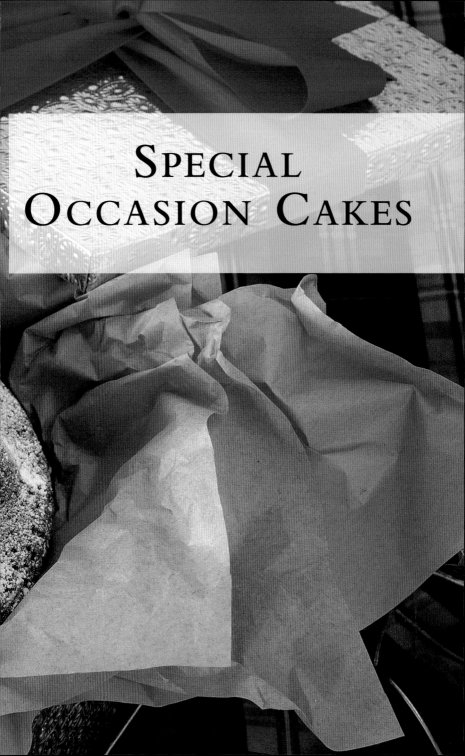

SPECIAL
OCCASION CAKES

Christening Sampler

Instead of embroidering a sampler to welcome a newborn baby, why not make a sampler cake to celebrate?

Serves 30

INGREDIENTS

1¼ x quantity rich fruit cake, baked in a
   20 cm/8 in square tin (pan)
45 ml/3 tbsp apricot glaze
1 x quantity marzipan
2 x quantity sugarpaste (fondant) icing
brown, yellow, orange, purple, cream, blue,
   green and pink food colouring

1 Brush the cake with apricot glaze. Roll out the marzipan, cover the cake and leave to dry overnight. Roll out 150 g/5 oz/1 cup of the sugarpaste icing to fit the cake top. Brush the top with water and cover with the icing.

2 Colour 300 g/11 oz/2 cups of the icing brown and roll out four pieces to the length and about 1 cm/½ in wider than the cake sides. Brush the sides with water and cover with icing, folding over the extra width at the top and cutting the corners at an angle to make a frame. Place on a cake board.

3 With a fine paintbrush, paint fine lines over the sides with watered-down brown food colouring to represent wood grain.

4 Take the remaining icing and colour small amounts yellow, orange, brown, purple and cream and two shades of blue, green and pink. Leave a little white.

5 Use these colours to shape the ducks, teddy bear, bulrushes, water, branch and leaves. Cut out a pink heart with a cookie cutter and make the baby's initial from white icing. Mix the white and pink icings together for the apple blossom flowers.

6 Make the shapes for the border. Attach the decorations to the cake with a little water. Use the leftover colours to make "threads". Arrange in loops around the base of the cake on the cake board.

Double Heart Engagement Cake

For a celebratory party, these sumptuous cakes make the perfect centrepiece.

Serves 20

INGREDIENTS
350 g/12 oz plain (semisweet) chocolate
2 x quantity chocolate-flavour
    quick-mix sponge cakes,
    baked in 20 cm/8 in
    heart-shaped tins (pans)
2 x quantity coffee-flavour
    butter icing
icing (confectioners') sugar, for dusting
fresh raspberries, to decorate

1 Melt the chocolate in a heatproof bowl over a pan of hot water (you may find it easier to work with half the chocolate at a time). Pour the chocolate on to a smooth, non-porous surface and spread it out with a metal spatula. Leave to cool slightly until just set, but not hard.

2 To make the chocolate curls, hold a large sharp knife at a 45° angle to the chocolate and push it along the chocolate in short sawing movements. Leave to set on baking parchment.

COOK'S TIP: The finished cakes can be kept for up to 3 days in an airtight container in the refrigerator.

3 Cut each cake in half horizontally. Use one-third of the butter icing to sandwich the cakes together. Use the remaining icing to coat the tops and sides of the cakes.

4 Place the cakes on heart-shaped cake boards. Generously cover the tops and sides of the cakes with the chocolate curls, pressing them gently into the butter icing.

5 Sift a little icing sugar over the top of each cake and decorate with raspberries. Chill until ready to serve.

Valentine's Box of Chocolates

This special cake would also make a wonderful gift for Mother's Day. Choose her favourite chocolates to go inside.

Serves 10–12

INGREDIENTS

1½ x quantity chocolate-flavour quick-mix sponge cake, baked in a 20 cm/8 in heart-shaped tin (pan)

⅔ x quantity marzipan

120 ml/4 fl oz/½ cup apricot glaze

3 x quantity sugarpaste (fondant) icing

red food colouring

length of ribbon tied in a bow, and a pin

225 g/8 oz/about 16–20 hand-made chocolates

small paper sweet (candy) cases

1 Place the cake on a 23 cm/9 in square piece of stiff card, draw around it, and cut the heart shape out to make a template. It will be used to support the box lid. Using a sharp knife, cut through the cake horizontally, just below the dome. Place the top section on the card and the base on a board. Use a piece of string to measure around the outside of the base.

2 Roll the marzipan into a long sausage to the measured length of the string. Place on the cake around the outside edge. Brush both sections of the cake with apricot glaze. Tint the sugarpaste icing red and cut off one-third. Cut another 50 g/2 oz/⅓ cup portion from the larger piece. Set aside. Use the large piece to cover the base section of cake.

3 Stand the lid on a raised surface. Use the reserved one-third of sugarpaste icing to cover the lid. Roll out the remaining piece of icing and stamp out small hearts with a cookie cutter. Stick them around the edge of the lid with water. Secure the ribbon bow on top of the lid with the pin.

4 Place the chocolates in the paper cases and arrange in the cake base. Position the lid slightly off-centre, to reveal the chocolates. **Do not forget to remove the ribbon and pin before serving the cake.**

Mother's Day Basket

Every mother would love to receive a cake like this on Mother's Day. Choose fresh flowers to decorate the top.

Serves 12

INGREDIENTS

1½ x quantity orange-flavour quick-mix sponge cake, baked in a fluted dish or brioche mould
3 x quantity orange-flavour butter icing
1 m/1 yd x 1 cm/½ in wide mauve ribbon
50 cm/20 in x 3 mm/⅛ in wide spotted mauve ribbon
fresh flowers

1 Spread the side of the cake with one-third of the butter icing and place upside down on a board.

2 Half fill a piping (icing) bag fitted with a basket-weave nozzle with butter icing. Pipe a vertical line down the side of the cake, then pipe four horizontal lines across the vertical line, starting at the top of the cake and equally spacing the lines apart.

3 Pipe another vertical line of icing on the edge of the horizontal lines, then pipe four horizontal lines across this between the spaces formed by the previous horizontal lines, to form a basket-weave. Continue until the sides are completely covered.

4 Invert the cake on to the cake board and spread the top with butter icing. Pipe a shell edging, using the basket-weave nozzle, to neaten the top edge. Continue to pipe the basket-weave icing across the top of the cake, starting at the edge. Leave the cake to set in a cool place.

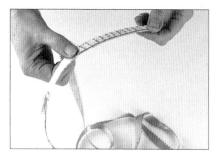

5 Fold a piece of foil in half, then half again and continue to fold until you have a strip several layers thick. Using the 1 cm/½ in wide mauve ribbon, bind the strip to cover the foil; bend up the end to secure the ribbon. Bend the foil to make a handle, and press into the icing.

6 Choose some flowers and make a neat arrangement tied with the spotted ribbon on top of the cake just before serving. Tie a bow and pin it to the sides of the cake.

COOK'S TIP: Wrap the flower stalks in silver paper, if liked.

Simnel Cake

This is a traditional Easter cake, but is delicious at any time of year.

Serves 10–12

INGREDIENTS
225 g/8 oz/1 cup butter, softened
225 g/8 oz/generous 1 cup caster
    (superfine) sugar
4 eggs, beaten
500 g/1¼ lb/3⅓ cups mixed dried fruit
115 g/4 oz/½ cup glacé (candied) cherries
45 ml/3 tbsp sherry (optional)
275 g/10 oz/2½ cups plain (all-purpose) flour
15 ml/1 tbsp mixed (apple pie) spice
5 ml/1 tsp baking powder
675 g/1½ lb/4½ cups yellow marzipan
1 egg yolk, beaten
ribbons, sugared eggs and sugarpaste
    animals, to decorate

1 Preheat the oven to 160°C/325°F/
Gas 3. Grease and line a deep
20 cm/8 in round cake tin (pan).

2 Beat the butter and sugar until
fluffy. Gradually beat in the eggs. Stir
in the fruit, cherries and sherry, if
using. Sift over the flour, mixed spice
and baking powder, then fold in.

3 Roll out half the marzipan to a
20 cm/8 in round. Spoon half the cake
mixture into the cake tin and place the
round of marzipan on top. Add the
other half of the cake mixture and
smooth the surface.

4 Bake for 2½ hours, or until golden
and springy to the touch. Leave in the
tin for 15 minutes, then turn out on to
a wire rack, peel off the lining paper
and leave to cool.

5 Roll out the reserved marzipan
to fit the cake. Brush the cake
top with egg yolk and place the
marzipan circle on top. Flute the
edges and make a lattice pattern on
top with a fork.

6 Brush the top of the marzipan with
more egg yolk. Put the cake on
a baking sheet and grill (broil) for
5 minutes to brown the top lightly.
Cool before decorating with ribbons,
sugared eggs and sugarpaste animals.

Hallowe'en Pumpkin

This is the time for spooky cakes, and witches may even burst out of them. Make the cake and butter icing your favourite flavour.

Serves 15

INGREDIENTS

1 x quantity Madeira cake, baked in two
    1.2 litre/2 pint/5 cup pudding bowls
1 x quantity orange-flavour butter icing
1½ x quantity sugarpaste (fondant) icing
orange, black and yellow food colouring
90 g/3½ oz/⅔ cup royal icing

1 Trim the widest ends of the cakes so that they will fit together. Split each cake in half horizontally, then sandwich the layers together with butter icing. Trim one end narrower for a better shape and to form the base. Cover the cake with the remaining butter icing.

2 Colour 350 g/12 oz/2¼ cups of the sugarpaste icing orange. Roll out and cover the cake, trimming to fit. Reserve the trimmings. Mark segments on the icing with a skewer. Paint the markings of pumpkin flesh with watered-down orange food colouring.

3 Cut and tear the sugarpaste trimmings into jagged pieces, to make the place where the witch bursts out. Attach to the cake with a little water.

4 Colour three-quarters of the remaining sugarpaste icing black. Colour a little of the remainder yellow and leave the rest white. Use black and white icing to make the witch's head, arms and body, joining them with royal icing.

5 Make the cape and hat from black icing. Shape the cauldron, broomstick and cat's head from black and yellow icing, securing the cauldron handle with royal icing when dry. Leave to dry.

6 Use a sharp knife to make the pumpkin features from the remaining black icing. Attach to the pumpkin with a little water. Secure the witch on the top of the cake with royal icing and arrange her accoutrements around the base.

Spiced Christmas Cake

This light cake mixture is flavoured with spices and fruit. It can be served with a dusting of icing sugar and decorated with holly leaves.

Serves 6–8

INGREDIENTS

225 g/8 oz/1 cup butter, plus 15 ml/1 tbsp
15 ml/1 tbsp fresh white breadcrumbs
225 g/8 oz/1 cup caster (superfine) sugar
50 ml/2 fl oz/¼ cup water
3 eggs, separated
225 g/8 oz/2 cups self-raising (self-rising) flour
7.5 ml/1½ tsp mixed (apple pie) spice
25 g/1 oz/2 tbsp chopped angelica
25 g/1 oz/2 tbsp mixed (candied) peel
50 g/2 oz/¼ cup glacé (candied) cherries
50 g/2 oz/½ cup walnuts, chopped
icing (confectioners') sugar, to dust

1 Preheat the oven to 180°C/350°F/ Gas 4. Brush a 20 cm/8 in, 1.5 litre/2½ pint/6¼ cup fluted ring mould with 15 ml/1 tbsp melted butter. Coat the greased ring mould with fresh white breadcrumbs, shaking to remove any excess crumbs.

2 Place the butter, sugar and water in a pan. Heat gently, stirring occasionally, until melted. Boil for 3 minutes, until syrupy, then set aside to cool.

3 Whisk the egg whites until stiff. Sift the flour and spice into a bowl, add the angelica, mixed peel, cherries and walnuts and stir well to mix. Add the egg yolks.

4 Pour the cooled syrup into the bowl and beat together with a wooden spoon to form a soft batter. Gradually fold in the egg whites, using a plastic spatula, until the mixture is evenly blended.

5 Pour into the mould and bake for 50–60 minutes, or until the cake springs back when pressed. Turn out and cool on a wire rack. Dust the cake thickly with icing sugar and decorate with a sprig of holly.

Christmas Stocking Cake

This charming fruit cake is easy to decorate in festive style.

Makes 1 x 20 cm/8 in
square cake

INGREDIENTS
1 x 20 cm/8 in square rich fruit cake
45 ml/3 tbsp apricot glaze
2 x quantity marzipan
4 x quantity sugarpaste (fondant) icing
15 ml/1 tbsp royal icing
red and green ribbons
red and green food colouring

1 Brush the cake with the apricot glaze and place on a 25 cm/10 in square cake board. Cover the cake with marzipan.

2 Set aside 225 g/8 oz/1½ cups of the sugarpaste icing. Cover the cake with the remainder and leave to dry. Secure the red ribbon around the board and the green ribbon around the cake with royal icing.

3 Divide the reserved sugarpaste icing in half and roll out one half. Using a template cut out two sugarpaste stockings, one 5 mm/¼ in larger all around. Put the smaller one on top of the larger one. Reserve the remaining white icing.

4 Divide the other half of the sugarpaste into two and tint one half red and the other green.

5 Roll out and cut seven 1 cm/½ in strips from each colour. Alternate the strips on top of the stocking. Roll lightly to fuse and press the edges together. Leave to dry.

6 Shape the remaining white sugarpaste into four parcels. Trim with red and green sugarpaste ribbons. Use the remaining red and green sugarpaste to make thin strips to decorate the cake sides. Secure in place with royal icing. Stick small sugarpaste balls over the joins. Arrange the stocking and parcels on the cake top.

PARTY CAKES AND
BAKES FOR KIDS

Monster Meringues

Children will be clamouring for more of these crisp, mouth-watering meringues, whipped cream and tangy summer fruits.

Serves 4

INGREDIENTS

3 egg whites
175 g/6 oz/¾ cup caster (superfine) sugar
15 ml/1 tbsp cornflour (cornstarch)
5 ml/1 tsp white wine vinegar
few drops of vanilla essence (extract)
225 g/8 oz/1½ cups assorted red
    summer fruits
300 ml/½ pint/1¼ cups double
    (heavy) cream
1 passion fruit

1 Preheat the oven to 140°C/275°F/ Gas 1. Using a pencil, draw eight 10 cm/4 in circles on two sheets of non-stick baking parchment which will fit on two baking sheets. Place the paper face-down on the baking sheets.

2 Whisk the egg whites until they are stiff, then gradually add the caster sugar, whisking well after each separate addition until the mixture has become very stiff.

3 Using a metal spoon, gently stir in the cornflour, vinegar and vanilla essence. Put the meringue mixture into a large piping (pastry) bag fitted with a large star nozzle.

4 Pipe a solid layer of meringue in four of the drawn circles and then pipe a lattice pattern in the other four. Cook in the oven for 1¼–1½ hours, swapping the shelf positions after 30 minutes, until lightly browned. The paper will peel off the back easily when the meringues are cooked. Allow to cool.

5 Roughly chop most of the summer fruits, reserving a few for decoration. Whip the cream and spread it over the solid meringue shapes. Scatter the chopped fruit on top. Halve the passion fruit, scoop out the seeds with a teaspoon and scatter them over. Top with a lattice lid and serve with the reserved whole fruits.

Kooky Cookies

Cut out these easy cookies in lots of different shapes and let your
imagination run wild with the decorating, using lots of bright colours.

Makes 20

INGREDIENTS
115 g/4 oz/1 cup self-raising
   (self-rising) flour
5 ml/1 tsp ground ginger
5 ml/1 tsp bicarbonate of soda (baking soda)
50 g/2 oz/¼ cup sugar
50 g/2 oz/¼ cup butter, softened
30 ml/2 tbsp golden (light corn) syrup

FOR THE ICING
115 g/4 oz/½ cup butter, softened
225 g/8 oz/2 cups icing (confectioners') sugar
5 ml/1 tsp lemon juice
few drops of food colouring
coloured writing icing
coloured sweets

1 Sift the self-raising flour, ground
ginger and bicarbonate of soda into a
large mixing bowl. Add the sugar, then
carefully rub in the softened butter
with your fingertips, lifting the
mixture above the bowl, until it
resembles fine breadcrumbs.

2 Add the golden syrup and mix to a
dough. Preheat the oven to 190°C/
375°F/Gas 5. Grease a baking sheet.

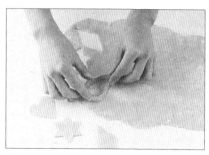

3 Roll out to 3 mm/⅛ in thick on a
lightly floured surface. Stamp out
shapes with cookie cutters and transfer
to the prepared baking sheet. Bake for
5–10 minutes before transferring to a
wire rack to cool.

4 To make the icing, beat the butter
in a bowl until light and fluffy. Add the
icing sugar a little at a time and
continue beating. Add the lemon juice
and food colouring. Spread over some
of the cooled cookies and leave to set.

5 To make each cookie individual, decorate some with coloured sweets just before the icing has set completely. Leave the other cookies until the icing has set and then decorate them with a variety of coloured writing icing.

Mint-surprise Chocolate Cupcakes

Exclamations of delight will be heard as children discover the creamy, mint filling that is hidden within these little cupcakes, which are also topped with minty chocolate icing.

Makes 12

INGREDIENTS
225 g/8 oz/2 cups plain (all-purpose) flour
5 ml/1 tsp bicarbonate of soda (baking soda)
pinch of salt
50 g/2 oz/½ cup unsweetened
   cocoa powder
150 g/5 oz/10 tbsp unsalted (sweet)
   butter, softened
300 g/11 oz/1½ cups caster
   (superfine) sugar
3 eggs
5 ml/1 tsp peppermint essence (extract)
250 ml/8 fl oz/1 cup milk

FOR THE MINT CREAM FILLING
300 ml/½ pint/1¼ cups double (heavy) or
   whipping cream
5 ml/1 tsp peppermint essence (extract)

FOR THE CHOCOLATE MINT GLAZE
175 g/6 oz plain (semisweet) chocolate
115 g/4 oz/½ cup unsalted (sweet) butter
5 ml/1 tsp peppermint essence (extract)

1 Preheat the oven to 180°C/350°F/
Gas 4. Line a 12-hole bun tray with
individual paper cases. Into a mixing
bowl, sift together the flour,
bicarbonate of soda, pinch of salt and
cocoa powder.

2 Using a hand-held electric mixer,
beat the butter and sugar in a large
mixing bowl until light and creamy.

3 Add the eggs to the butter and
sugar one at a time, beating well after
each addition, then beat in the
peppermint essence. On low speed,
beat in the flour mixture alternately
with the milk until just blended.
Spoon into the prepared paper cases.

4 Bake for 12–15 minutes until a thin
skewer inserted in the centre of a bun
comes out clean: do not over-bake.

5 Immediately remove the cupcakes
from the tin to a wire rack to cool
completely. When they are cool,
remove the paper cases.

6 To make the filling, whip the cream and peppermint essence in a small bowl until stiff peaks form. Spoon into a small icing bag fitted with a small, plain tip. Push the tip into the bottom of a cupcake and squeeze gently, releasing about 15 ml/1 tbsp of cream into the centre. Repeat with the remaining cupcakes.

7 To make the glaze, melt the chocolate and butter in a pan over low heat, stirring until smooth. Remove from the heat and stir in the peppermint essence. Cool, then spread on top of each cake.

Chunky Choc Bars

An easy cake that needs no cooking and is a smash-hit with kids.

Makes 12

INGREDIENTS
350 g/12 oz plain (semisweet) chocolate
115 g/4 oz/½ cup butter
400 g/14 oz can evaporated (unsweetened condensed) milk
225 g/8 oz digestive biscuits (graham crackers), broken
50 g/2 oz/⅓ cup raisins
115 g/4 oz/⅔ cup dried peaches, chopped
50 g/2 oz/½ cup hazelnuts or pecans, chopped

2 Beat the evaporated milk into the chocolate and butter mixture. Add the biscuits, raisins, peaches and nuts and mix well until all the ingredients are coated in chocolate.

3 Turn the mixture into the prepared tin, making sure it is pressed well into the corners. Leave the top craggy. Put in the refrigerator and leave to set.

1 Line an 18 x 28 cm/7 x 11 in cake tin (pan) with clear film (plastic wrap). Put the chocolate and butter in a large bowl over a pan of hot but not boiling water and leave to melt. Stir until well mixed.

VARIATION: Experiment with different fruits and nuts. Try replacing the peaches with chopped dried apples and the chopped hazelnuts or pecans with toasted blanched almonds.

4 Lift the cake out of the tin using the clear film and then carefully peel it off. Cut the cake into 12 bars and keep chilled until ready to serve.

Drum

This is a colourful cake for very young children, who will find it so realistic that they may want to play it!

Makes a 15 cm/6 in round cake

INGREDIENTS
15 cm/6 in round quick-mix sponge cake
50 g/2 oz/¼ cup butter icing
apricot glaze
350 g/12 oz/2¼ cups marzipan
1¼ x quantity sugarpaste (fondant) icing
red, blue and yellow
    food colourings

1 Split the cake and fill with the butter icing. Place on a 20 cm/8 in round cake board and brush with the hot apricot glaze.

2 Cover the cake with a layer of marzipan and leave it to dry overnight.

3 Colour half the sugarpaste icing red. Reserve a small amount for the drumsticks, then roll out to 25 x 30 cm/10 x 12 in and cut in half. Stick to the sides of the cake with water, smoothing the joins neatly.

4 Reserve a little white icing for the drumsticks, then roll out a circle to fit the top of the cake.

5 Divide the rest of the sugarpaste icing in half. Colour one half blue and the other yellow. Divide the blue into four equal pieces and roll each piece into a sausage long enough to go half way round the cake. Stick around the base and top of the cake with water.

6 Using a sharp knife, mark the blue edging of the cake into six around the top and bottom using a circle of baking parchment that has been folded to show six wedges.

7 Roll the yellow fondant icing into strands long enough to cross diagonally from top to bottom to form the drum strings. Roll the rest of the yellow fondant icing into 12 small balls and stick where the strings join the drum.

8 Using the remaining red and white fondant icing, knead together until streaky and roll two balls and sticks 15 cm/6 in long. Dry overnight. Stick together with a little royal icing to make the drumsticks.

Banjo Cake

The perfect cake for a musical child. It can be set on a large tray or you could cut out a card template to support it.

Serves 15–20

INGREDIENTS
2 x quantity quick-mix sponge cake,
   baked in one 20 cm/8 in round tin (pan)
   and one 18 cm/7 in square tin
115 g/4 oz/6 tbsp seedless raspberry
   jam, warmed
2⅔ x quantity sugarpaste (fondant) icing
lime green food colouring
2 coloured sticks of liquorice
4 round lollipops
60 ml/4 tbsp coloured vermicelli
pieces of flat green liquorice
2 long red liquorice bootlaces
4 long green liquorice bootlaces
ribbon and 2 pins, for the strap
sugarpaste stars (optional)

1 Cut the dome off the round cake and place bottom side up. Cut the dome off the square cake, then cut in half down the middle. Place together in a banjo shape. Draw round them on stiff card and cut out to make a reinforcing template.

2 Stamp out a shallow hole in the round cake with a 5 cm/2 in cutter. Place the cakes on the base and brush with the jam.

3 Colour the sugarpaste icing lime green and roll out to a 62 x 25 cm/ 25 x 10 in rectangle. Cover the banjo, easing the icing into the hollow and down the sides. Make finger indentations along the length of the neck on each side.

4 Cut off four 1 cm/½ in pieces from 1 liquorice stick and press into the top end of the banjo neck. Place the remaining piece and the other liquorice stick next to the hollow. Dip the lollipops in water and then in the coloured vermicelli. Press them into the sides of the neck end to line up with the liquorice.

5 Place the flat liquorice pieces side by side at the base, securing with a little water. Cut the red bootlace into 5 cm/2 in lengths. Position them along the neck to make frets, securing with water if necessary.

> COOK'S TIP: The finished cake can be made up to 2 days in advance and kept in a cool, dry place.

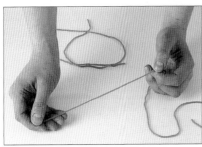

6 Dip the green bootlaces in hot water and stretch until straight. Wrap one end of the bootlace strings around the liquorice sticks and attach the other ends to the flat liquorice pieces. Secure the ribbon strap with pins and decorate the banjo with sugarpaste stars, if wished. **Do not forget to remove the pins before serving.**

Teddy's Birthday

Young children will adore this jolly-faced teddy bear with his own cake.

Makes a 20 cm/8 in round cake

INGREDIENTS
20 cm/8 in round quick-mix sponge cake
115 g/4 oz/1¼ cups butter icing
apricot glaze
350 g/12 oz/2½ cups marzipan
1¼ x quantity sugarpaste (fondant) icing
brown, pink, red, blue and black
    food colourings
115 g/4 oz/¾ cup royal icing
silver balls
1.5 m/1½ yds ribbon, 2.5 cm/1 in wide, and
    candles, to decorate

1 Split the cake and fill with the butter icing. Place on a 25 cm/10 in round cake board and brush with hot apricot glaze. Cover with a layer of marzipan, then sugarpaste icing. Using a template, mark the design on top of the cake.

2 Colour one-third of the remaining sugarpaste icing pale brown. Colour a piece pink, a piece red, some blue and a tiny piece black. Using a template, cut out the pieces to make the teddy.

3 Place the pieces in position. Stick down by lifting the edges and brushing the undersides with water. Roll ovals for the eyes and stick in place with the nose and eyebrows. Cut out a mouth and press flat.

4 Tie the ribbon around the cake. Colour the royal icing blue and pipe a border around the base of the cake using a no. 7 shell tube.

5 Pipe tiny stars around the small cake using a no. 7 star tube and inserting silver balls. Place the candles on the small cake.

COOK'S TIP: For a 20 cm/8 in round cake, follow the instructions for the 15 cm/6 in cake, but use three eggs, 175 g/6 oz/¾ cup caster (superfine) sugar, 175 g/6 oz/¾ cup butter or margarine, 175 g/6 oz/1½ cups self-raising (self-rising) flour, 4 ml/¾ tsp baking powder and 30 ml/2 tbsp water. Bake for 45–55 minutes.

Ballerina

This cake requires patience and plenty of time for the decoration.

Makes a 20 cm/8 in round cake

INGREDIENTS
20 cm/8 in round quick-mix sponge cake
115 g/4 oz/1¼ cups butter icing
apricot glaze
450 g/1 lb/3 cups marzipan
1¼ x quantity sugarpaste (fondant) icing
pink, green, yellow, brown and blue
    food colourings
115 g/4 oz/¾ cup royal icing
1.5 m/1½ yds ribbon, 2.5 cm/1 in wide

1 Split the cake and fill with the butter icing. Place on a 25 cm/10 in round cake board and brush with hot apricot glaze. Cover with a layer of marzipan then a layer of sugarpaste icing. Leave to dry overnight.

2 Divide the remaining sugarpaste icing into three; colour one flesh tones and the other two contrasting pinks. Roll out each colour and use 5 mm/ ¼ in and 9 mm/⅜ in flower cutters with ejectors to cut out 12 flowers and three tiny flowers from the paler pink fondant. Set aside to dry.

3 Using a template, carefully mark the position of the ballerina. Cut out the body from flesh-coloured icing and stick in position with water. Round off the edges gently with a finger. Cut out a bodice from the darker pink sugarpaste and stick in place.

4 To make the tutu, work swiftly as the thin sugarpaste dries quickly and will crack. Roll out the darker pink sugarpaste to 3 mm/⅛ in thick and cut out a fluted circle with a small plain inner circle. Cut into quarters and, with a cocktail stick (toothpick), roll along the fluted edge to stretch it.

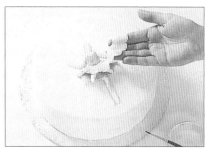

5 Attach the frills to the waist with a little water. Repeat with two more layers, using a cocktail stick to shape the frills and cotton wool to hold them in place until dry. For the final layer of frills, use the paler pink sugarpaste and cover with a short dark frill, as the bodice extension. Leave to dry overnight.

6 Attach flowers as the hoop. Colour a little royal icing green and pipe tiny leaves. Paint on the face and hair. Stick tiny flowers around the head. Cut pale pink shoes and stick on, and paint ribbons. Pipe the flower centres from dark pink royal icing. Pipe royal icing around the base with a no. 7 shell tube. Tie with pink ribbon, to decorate.

COOK'S TIP: For this size cake, follow the steps for the 15 cm/6 in cake, but use three eggs, 175 g/6 oz/ ¾ cup sugar, 175 g/6 oz/¾ cup butter or margarine, 175 g/6 oz/ 1½ cups flour, 4 ml/¾ tsp baking powder and 30 ml/2 tbsp water. Bake for 45–55 minutes.

Child's Fairy Cake

Allow yourself plenty of time for decorating this enchanting novelty cake.

Serves 6–8

INGREDIENTS
1 x quantity quick-mix sponge cake mix
⅓ x quantity butter icing
30 ml/2 tbsp apricot glaze
1 x quantity marzipan
⅛ x quantity royal icing
pink sparkle lustre powder
silver balls

FOR THE SUGARPASTE ICING
450 g/1 lb/4 cups icing
   (confectioners') sugar
1 egg white
27½ ml/5½ tsp liquid glucose
blue, pink, yellow and gold food colouring

1 Preheat the oven to 160°C/325°F/ Gas 3. Grease and line a 20 cm/8 in round cake tin (pan). Spoon in the mixture, smooth the surface and bake for 30-40 minutes, until a skewer inserted in the centre comes out clean. Turn out and cool on a wire rack.

2 To make the sugarpaste icing, put the icing sugar, egg white and glucose in a food processor or mixer and process until the mixture resembles fine breadcrumbs. Knead well until smooth and pliable, adding a drop of water if it is too dry. Set aside 50 g/ 2 oz/¼ cup in a plastic bag in the refrigerator and colour the remainder pale blue, kneading well.

3 Cut the cake in half horizontally and sandwich together with the butter icing. Place on a 25 cm/10 in round cake board and brush with the glaze. Roll out the marzipan and use to cover the cake. Roll out the blue sugarpaste icing and use to cover the cake. Leave to dry overnight.

4 Using a template, mark the position of the fairy. Spoon the royal icing into a piping bag with a No. 1 nozzle and pipe the outline of each wing. Pipe a second line inside the first. With a damp paint brush, brush long strokes in from the edges, leaving more icing at the edges and fading away to a thin film near the base. Leave to dry for 1 hour. Brush with dry lustre powder.

5 Colour a little of the white sugarpaste icing flesh colour. Roll out and cut out the body. Stick on the cake with a little water. Round sharp edges with your finger. Cut out the bodice and shoes and stick in place. Cut out a wand and star and leave to dry.

6 Make the tutu frills one at a time. Roll out a small piece of sugarpaste to 3 mm/⅛ in thick and stamp out a circle with a small fluted cutter. Cut it into quarters and roll a cocktail stick (toothpick) along the fluted edge to stretch it and give fullness.

7 Stick one frill to the waist. Repeat with the other layers, tucking the sides in neatly. Use a cocktail stick to arrange the frills and support the folds with small pieces of cotton wool until dry.

8 Brush a little lustre powder over the edge of the tutu. Paint on the hair and face, stick on the wand and star and paint the star gold. Pipe a border of royal icing around the board using a No. 7 star nozzle and place a silver ball on alternate points. Leave to dry.

9 Colour a little royal icing yellow and pipe over the hair. Paint with a touch of gold colouring.

Mermaid Cake

Pretty, elegant and flavoured with delicious chocolate, this cake must be every little girl's dream. The cake can be filled with butter icing.

Serves 6–8

INGREDIENTS

1 x quantity chocolate-flavour quick-mix
   sponge cake, baked in a
   900 g/2 lb loaf tin (pan)
450 g/1 lb plain (semisweet) chocolate
25 g/1 oz/3 cups
   unflavoured popcorn
1½ x quantity sugarpaste (fondant) icing
lilac and pink
   food colouring
1 Barbie- or Sindy-type doll
45 ml/3 tbsp apricot glaze,
   plus a little extra
1 egg white, lightly beaten
demerara (raw) sugar
sea shells (optional)

1 Place the cake on a cake board. Melt the chocolate over a pan of simmering water. Stir in the popcorn until evenly coated, then spoon around the sides of the cake and on the board. Spread any remaining melted chocolate over the top of the cake.

2 Colour about three-quarters of the sugarpaste icing lilac and the remainder pink. Reserve the pink icing and one-third of the lilac icing wrapped in clear film (plastic wrap). Roll out the remaining lilac icing to a rectangle wide enough to wrap around the doll's legs and about 5 cm/2 in longer.

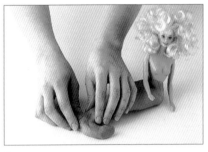

3 Brush the doll from the waist down with the apricot glaze, then wrap her in the sugarpaste, lightly squeezing and pinching to make it stick. Pinch the end of the tail to form a fin shape, curling the ends slightly. Position the mermaid on the cake.

4 Roll out the remaining lilac and the pink sugarpaste icing and stamp out scales with a small crescent-shaped cutter. Cover with clear film to prevent them from drying out. Starting at the fin, brush the crescents with a tiny amount of egg white and stick them to the tail, overlapping them, until it is completely covered.

5 Cut a shell-shaped bra top from the trimmings. Make indentations with the back of a knife and secure in place with a little apricot glaze.

6 Scatter demerara sugar around the base of the cake for sand and add a few real shells, if you like. Remove the doll before serving.

Racing Track

A cake to thrill all eight-year-old racing-car enthusiasts. It is relatively simple to make and can be decorated with as many cars as you like.

Makes 1 cake

INGREDIENTS
2 x 15 cm/6 in round quick-mix sponge
   cakes
½ x quantity butter icing
1½ x quantity sugarpaste (fondant) icing
blue and red food colourings
apricot glaze
1 quantity marzipan
⅙ x quantity royal icing
candles and 2 small racing cars,
   to decorate

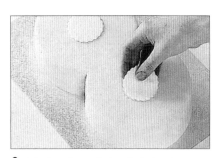

3 Mark a 5 cm/2 in circle in the centre of each cake. Roll out the remaining white sugarpaste icing, cut out two fluted circles and stick in the marked spaces.

4 Colour the royal icing red. Pipe a shell border around the base of the cake using a no. 8 star tube.

1 Split the cakes and fill with the butter icing. Cut off a 1 cm/½ in piece from one side of each cake and then place both the cakes on a 25 x 35 cm/ 10 x 14 in cake board with the flat edges together.

2 Colour about 450 g/1 lb/4½ cups of the sugarpaste icing pale blue. Brush the cakes with hot apricot glaze. Cover with a layer of marzipan, then with the pale blue sugarpaste icing.

5 Pipe a track for the cars on the cake using a no. 2 plain tube. Place the candles on the two white circles and arrange the cars on the track.

Computer Game

The perfect cake to bake for a computer game fanatic.

Makes 1 cake

INGREDIENTS
15 cm/6 in square quick-mix sponge cake
115 g/4 oz/1¼ cups butter icing
apricot glaze
1 x quantity sugarpaste
  (fondant) icing
black, blue, red and yellow
  food colourings
225 g/8 oz/1½ cups marzipan
¼ x quantity royal icing

1 Split the cake and fill with the butter icing. With a sharp, serrated knife, cut 2.5 cm/1 in off one side of the cake and 1 cm/½ in off the other. Round the corners slightly. Place on a 20 cm/8 in square cake board and brush with hot apricot glaze.

2 Colour 225 g/8 oz/1½ cups of the sugarpaste icing black. Cover the cake with a layer of marzipan, then with most of the black sugarpaste icing.

3 With a wooden cocktail stick (toothpick), mark the speaker holes and position of the screen and knobs.

4 Colour half the remaining white sugarpaste icing pale blue, roll out and cut out a 6 cm/2½ in square for the screen. Stick in the centre of the game with a little water.

5 Colour a small piece of sugarpaste icing red and the rest yellow. Cut out the start switch 2.5 cm/1 in long from the red and the controls from the yellow. Stick into position with water.

6 Roll the remaining black sugarpaste into a long, thin sausage and use it to edge the screen and around the base of the cake.

7 With a fine paintbrush, draw the game on to the screen with a little blue colour. Pipe letters on to the buttons with a little royal icing.

Smiley Kite

The face on this happy kite is a great favourite with children of all ages.

Makes 1 cake

INGREDIENTS
25 cm/10 in square quick-mix sponge cake
225 g/8 oz/2⅓ cups butter icing
apricot glaze
2 x quantity sugarpaste (fondant) icing
yellow, red, green, blue and black
    food colourings
450 g/1 lb/3 cups marzipan
115 g/4 oz/¾ cup royal icing

1 Split the cake and fill with the butter icing. Mark 15 cm/6 in from one corner down two sides and, guided by a ruler, cut down to the opposite corner on both sides. Place diagonally on a 30 cm/12 in square cake board and brush with hot apricot glaze.

2 Colour 450 g/1 lb/3 cups of the sugarpaste icing pale yellow. Divide the remainder into five portions leaving one white and colour the other four red, green, blue and black. Wrap each piece in clear film (plastic wrap).

3 Cover the cake with a layer of marzipan, then a layer of the yellow fondant, leaving some for the tail.

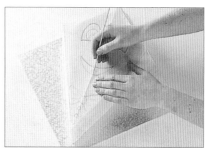

4 Using a template, mark the happy face on the kite. Pipe a shell border around the base of the cake. Cut out the face, bow tie and buttons from the different colours of fondant icing and stick in place with a little water.

5 To make the kite's tail, roll out each colour separately and cut two 4 x 1 cm/ 1½ x ½ in lengths from the blue, red and green fondants. Pinch them to shape into bows.

COOK'S TIP: For the cake, follow the steps for the 15 cm/6 in round cake, but use 8 eggs, 450 g/1 lb/2¼ cups caster (superfine) sugar, 450 g/ 1 lb/2 cups butter or margarine, 450 g/1 lb/4 cups self-raising (self-rising) flour, 10 ml/2 tsp baking powder and 105 ml/ 7 tbsp water. Bake for 1½–1¾ hours.

6 Roll most of the remaining yellow into a long rope and lay it on the board in a wavy line from the narrow end of the kite, then stick the bows in place with water. Roll balls of yellow fondant, stick on the board with a little royal icing and press in candles.

Dumper Truck

Any large round biscuits will work well for the wheels and all sorts of coloured sweets can go into the truck.

Serves 8–10

INGREDIENTS
1½ x quantity quick-mix sponge cake mix
90 ml/6 tbsp apricot glaze
2⅔ x quantity sugarpaste (fondant) icing
yellow, red and blue food colouring
about 12 sandwich wafer biscuits
4 coconut swirl cookies
115 g/4 oz coloured sweets (candies)
5 cm/2 in piece blue liquorice stick
demerara (raw) sugar, for the sand

1 Preheat the oven to 180°C/350°F/ Gas 4. Grease and line a 900 g/2 lb/ 5 cup loaf tin (pan). Spoon the cake mixture into the tin, smooth the surface and bake for 40–45 minutes, until a metal skewer inserted into the centre comes out clean. Transfer to a wire rack to cool.

2 Cut off the top of the cake. Cut off one-third of the cake for the cabin. Holding the larger piece cut side up, cut a hollow in the centre, leaving a 1 cm/½ in border. Brush with glaze.

3 Colour 350 g/12 oz/2¼ cups of the icing yellow. Set aside a piece the size of a walnut. Roll out the remainder on a surface lightly dusted with icing (confectioners') sugar to 5 mm/¼ in thick. Use to cover the larger piece of cake. Trim the bottom edges.

4 Colour 350 g/12 oz/2¼ cups of the remaining icing red. Set aside one-third and roll out the remainder to 5 mm/¼ in thick. Brush the remaining piece of cake with glaze, cover with the icing and trim the edges.

5 Break off and set aside a piece of the reserved red icing the size of a walnut and roll out the remainder. Brush an 18 x 7.5 cm/7 x 3 in piece of cake card with glaze and cover with the icing.

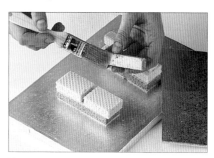

6 Brush the wafers with glaze and stick together in two equal piles. Place them on a 30 x 18 cm/12 x 7 in cake board about 7.5 cm/3 in apart. Place the covered cake card on top.

7 Place a little of the remaining white icing about halfway along the card. Place the dumper, slightly tilted, on top and the red cabin in front. Stand the coconut cookies in position for wheels.

8 Roll out the reserved yellow icing to a 5 x 2.5 cm/2 x 1 in rectangle. Colour the remaining icing blue and roll out thinly. Stamp out eyes with a crescent cutter. Roll out the reserved red icing and stamp out a mouth. Stick the yellow panel to the front of the cabin with water and stick on the features. Fill the dumper with sweets and push a piece of liquorice into the top of the cabin. Scatter the sugar around the truck to make sand.

Train Cake

This quick-and-easy train cake is made from a shaped tin, so all you need to do is decorate it!

Serves 8–10

INGREDIENTS

1½ x quantity quick-mix sponge cake, baked
   in a train-shaped tin (pan),
   about 35 cm/14 in long
2 x quantity butter icing
yellow food colouring
red liquorice bootlaces
90–120 ml/6–8 tbsp
   coloured vermicelli
4 liquorice wheels
pink and white cotton wool balls

1 Slice off the top surface of the cake to make it flat. Place diagonally on a cake board.

2 Tint the butter icing yellow. Use half of it to cover the cake.

COOK'S TIP: If you can't find a train-shaped tin (pan), cook the cake mix in a 23 cm/9 in square tin and cut out the shape.

3 Using a round nozzle and a quarter of the remaining butter icing, pipe a straight border around the top edge of the cake.

4 Place the red liquorice bootlaces on the piped border. Shape the bootlaces around the curves of the train to make a border. Pipe another butter-icing border inside the first border.

5 Using a small star nozzle and the remaining butter icing, pipe small stars over the top of the cake. Add extra liquorice and pipe other details, if you like. Use a metal spatula to press on the coloured vermicelli all around the sides of the cake.

6 Press the liquorice wheels in place for the wheels of the train. Pull a couple of balls of cotton wool apart for the steam and stick on to the cake board with butter icing.

Lion Cake

This spectacular cake is surprisingly easy to make and would be perfect for an animal lover or a Leo.

Serves 10–15

INGREDIENTS
1½ x quantity quick-mix sponge cake mix
1 x quantity orange-flavoured butter icing
orange and red food colouring
1½ x quantity yellow marzipan
⅙ x quantity sugarpaste (fondant) icing
red or orange liquorice bootlaces
long and round marshmallows

1 Preheat the oven to 180°C/350°F/ Gas 4. Grease and line a 25 x 30 cm/ 10 x 12 in tin (pan). Spoon in the cake mixture, smooth the top and bake for 45–50 minutes, until a metal skewer inserted into the centre comes out clean. Leave in the tin for 5 minutes, then turn out on to a wire rack to cool.

2 Place the cake base side up and cut an uneven scallop design around the edge. Turn the cake over and trim the top so that it sits squarely. Place it on a 30 cm/12 in square cake board.

3 Colour the butter icing orange and spread it evenly over the surface and down the sides of the cake.

4 Roll out 115 g/4 oz/¾ cup of the marzipan on a surface lightly dusted with icing (confectioners') sugar to a 15 cm/6 in square. Place in the centre of the cake, pressing down to secure.

5 Grate the remaining marzipan on to baking parchment. With a metal spatula, gently press it on to the cake to cover the sides and the top up to the edges of the face panel.

6 Colour the sugarpaste icing red and roll out on a surface lightly dusted with icing sugar. Stamp out a nose using a heart-shaped cutter and stick on the cake with a little water. With your fingers, roll two thin short strands for the mouth and stick on the cake.

7 Cut the liquorice bootlaces into lengths for the whiskers and place on the cake. Flatten two round marshmallows for eyes and stick on the cake with a little water. Cut the long marshmallows into 5 cm/2 in lengths and snip along one side to make the eyebrows. Stick on the cake with a little water.

Merry-go-round Cake

Choose your own figures to sit on the merry-go-round, from chocolate animals to jelly bears.

Serves 16–20

INGREDIENTS

1⅓ x quantity lemon-flavoured quick-mix sponge cake mix
60 ml/4 tbsp apricot glaze
1⅔ x quantity sugarpaste (fondant) icing
orange and yellow food colouring
8 x 18 cm/7 in long candy sticks
sweet (candy) figures

1 Preheat the oven to 180°C/350°F/ Gas 4. Grease and line two 20 cm/8 in round sandwich tins (pans). Spoon two-thirds of the cake mixture into one tin and the rest into the other, smooth the top and bake for 30–60 minutes, until a metal skewer inserted into the centres comes out clean. Leave in the tins for 5 minutes, then turn on to a wire rack.

2 Place the larger cake upside down on a 23 cm/9 in round fluted cake board. Place the smaller cake right side up on an 18 cm/7 in round piece of stiff card. Brush both with the glaze.

3 Roll out two-thirds of the icing on a surface dusted with icing (confectioners') sugar. Add a few spots of orange food colouring with a cocktail stick (toothpick). Roll the icing into a sausage shape, fold in half and roll out again. Repeat until it is streaked.

4 Roll out two-thirds of the orange icing and cover the larger cake. Roll out the remaining orange icing and cover the smaller cake. Trim and reserve the trimmings.

5 Using a candy stick, make eight holes evenly around the edge of the larger cake, leaving a 2 cm/¾ in border. Press the stick right through the cake to the board.

6 Knead the reserved orange icing until evenly coloured, then roll out thinly. Stamp out nine stars with a small star-shaped cutter and reserve.

7 Colour the remaining icing yellow. Roll it out and stamp out nine stars with a larger star-shaped cutter. Place the smaller cake on an upturned bowl and stick eight large and eight small stars around the edge with a little water. Stick the remaining stars on top.

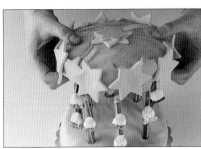

8 Secure the sweet figures to the candy sticks with reserved icing trimmings. Leave them to set for 30 minutes. Place the candy sticks in the holes in the larger cake. Assemble the cake just before serving. Lift the smaller cake, with its card base, on to the candy sticks, making sure it balances before letting go.

Indian Elephant

You can also make this delightful pachyderm for someone who loves to travel. Be as colourful as you like with the decoration.

Serves 30

INGREDIENTS
1¾ x quantity Madeira cake mix
2 x quantity butter icing
½ x quantity marzipan
black, green, yellow and pink
   food colouring
chocolate coins
silver balls
brown and white
   chocolate buttons
2 flat, round-shaped sweets (candies)
115 g/4 oz/2 cups desiccated (dry
   unsweetened shredded) coconut
30 ml/2 tbsp apricot glaze

1 Preheat the oven to 160°C/325°F/ Gas 3. Grease and line a 30 cm/12 in square cake tin (pan). Spoon in the mixture, tap lightly to level the surface and bake for 1½ hours, until a metal skewer inserted into the centre comes out clean. Place the tin on a wire rack for 10 minutes, then turn the cake out on to the rack to cool.

2 Make a template from stiff paper in the shape of an elephant and place on top of the cake. Cut out the shape with a sharp knife and transfer to a 35 cm/14 in cake board.

3 Colour the icing pale grey and cover the top and sides of the cake. Swirl with a metal spatula. Swirl black food colouring highlights into the icing with a cocktail stick (toothpick).

4 Roll out half the marzipan on a surface lightly dusted with icing (confectioners') sugar. Cut out shapes for the tusk, headpiece and blanket. Colour the remaining marzipan green, yellow and pink. Roll and cut out patterns for the blanket, headpiece, trunk and tail. Roll small balls of yellow and pink marzipan for the anklets.

5 Place the patterns and decorations in position. Cut the white chocolate buttons in half for toenails and make an eye from the sweets.

6 Colour the desiccated coconut green. Brush the cake board with the apricot glaze and sprinkle with the coconut.

Mouse in Bed

This cake is suitable for almost any age. Make the mouse well ahead to allow it time to dry.

Serves 8–10

INGREDIENTS

1 x quantity quick-mix sponge cake, baked in a 20 cm/8 in square tin (pan)
⅓ x quantity butter icing
45 ml/3 tbsp apricot glaze
1 x quantity marzipan
2 x quantity sugarpaste (fondant) icing
blue and pink food colouring and pens

1 Cut 5 cm/2 in off one side of the cake. Split and fill the main cake with butter icing. Place on a cake board. With the cake off-cut, shape a hollowed pillow, the torso and the legs of the mouse. Brush the cake with apricot glaze and cover with marzipan. Cover the pillow and mouse's torso and legs in the same way. Leave to dry overnight.

2 Cover the cake and pillow with white sugarpaste icing. Lightly frill the edge of the pillow with a fork.

3 To make the valance, roll out 350 g/ 12 oz/2¼ cups of sugarpaste icing and cut into four 7.5 cm/3 in wide strips. Attach to the bed with water. Arrange the pillow and mouse's body on the cake.

4 For the quilt, tint 75 g/3 oz/½ cup of sugarpaste icing blue and roll out to an 18 cm/7 in square. Mark with a diamond pattern and with a flower cutter. Cover the mouse with the quilt.

5 Cut a 2.5 x 18 cm/1 x 7 in white sugarpaste icing strip for the sheet, mark the edge and place over the quilt, tucking it under at the top edge.

6 Tint 25 g/1 oz/2 tbsp of marzipan pink and make the head and paws of the mouse. Put the head on the pillow, tucked under the sheet, and the paws over the edge of the sheet. Use food colouring pens to draw on the face of the mouse.

Number 7 Cake

Any combination of colours will work well for this marbled cake.

Serves 8–10

INGREDIENTS

1½ x quantity quick-mix sponge cake, baked
   in a 23 x 30 cm/9 x 12 in tin (pan)
1 x quantity orange-flavour butter icing
60 ml/4 tbsp apricot glaze
2 x quantity sugarpaste (fondant) icing
blue and green food colouring
rice paper sweets (candies)

4 Immediately after covering, use a
small "7" cutter to remove sugarpaste
shapes in a random pattern from the
covered cake.

1 Place the cake flat side up and cut
out the number seven. Slice the cake
horizontally, sandwich together with
the butter icing and place on a board.

2 Brush the cake evenly with apricot
glaze. Divide the sugarpaste icing into
three and tint one of the pieces blue
and another green. Set aside 50 g/
2 oz/⅓ cup from each of the
coloured icings.

3 Knead together the large pieces of
blue and green icing with the third
piece of white icing to marble. Use to
cover the cake.

5 Roll out the reserved blue and
green sugarpaste icing and stamp out
shapes with the same cutter. Use these
to fill the stamped-out shapes from the
cake. Decorate the board with some
rice paper sweets.

COOK'S TIP: If you are unsure
about shaping the number seven
cake freehand, you can purchase or
hire shaped cake tins from specialist
cake decorating shops.

Ladybird Cake

Children will love this colourful and appealing ladybird (ladybug), and it is very simple to make.

Serves 10–12

INGREDIENTS
1½ x quantity quick-mix sponge cake, baked in a 1.2 litre/2 pint/5 cup pudding bowl
½ x quantity butter icing
60 ml/4 tbsp lemon curd, warmed
3 x quantity sugarpaste (fondant) icing
red, black and green food colouring
5 marshmallows
50 g/2 oz/4 tbsp marzipan
2 pipe cleaners

1 Cut the cake in half horizontally and sandwich together with the butter icing. Cut vertically through the cake, about a third of the way in. Brush both pieces with the lemon curd. Colour 450 g/1 lb/3 cups of the sugarpaste icing red. Roll out to 5 mm/¼ in thick and cover the larger piece of cake to make the body. Using a skewer, make an indentation down the centre for the wings.

2 Colour 350 g/12 oz/2¼ cups of the icing black, roll out three-quarters and use to cover the smaller piece of cake for the head. Place both cakes on a cake board and press together.

3 Roll out 50 g/2 oz/⅓ cup of icing and cut out two 5 cm/2 in rounds for the eyes, then stick to the head with water. Roll out the remaining black icing and cut out eight 4 cm/1½ in rounds. Use two of these for the eyes and stick the others on to the body.

4 Place the ladybird on a cake board. Colour some icing green and squeeze through a garlic crusher to make grass. Flatten the marshmallows, snip and stick a marzipan round in the centre of each. Colour pipe cleaners black and press a ball of black icing on to the end of each. Arrange the grass and flowers around the ladybird. If you have sufficient trimmings, make baby ladybirds as well, if you like.

Index